WITHOUT AN ALPHABET, WITHOUT A FACE

Without an Alphabet, Without a Face

SELECTED POEMS BY

Saadi Youssef

Translated from the Arabic by Khaled Mattawa

Graywolf Press

SAINT PAUL, MINNESOTA

Publication of this volume is made possible in part by a grant provided by the
Minnesota State Arts Board, through an appropriation by the Minnesota State
Legislature, a grant from the Wells Fargo Foundation Minnesota, and a grant
from the National Endowment for the Arts. Significant support has also been
provided by the Bush Foundation; Marshall Field's Project Imagine with sup-
port from the Target Foundation; the McKnight Foundation; and other gen-
erous contributions from foundations, corporations, and individuals. To these
organizations and individuals we offer our heartfelt thanks.

A Lannan Translation Selection
Funding the translation and publication of exceptional literary works

Published by Graywolf Press
2402 University Avenue, Suite 203
Saint Paul, MN 55114
All rights reserved.

www.graywolfpress.org

Published in the United States of America

ISBN: 1-55597-371-x

2 4 6 8 9 7 5 3

Library of Congress Control Number: 2002102976

Cover design: Jeenee Lee Design

Cover art: Sawsan Amer, Egypt, *Icon* (detail), photographed by Mark Gulezian
Courtesy Database: The International Council for Women in the Arts/CVAR

ACKNOWLEDGMENTS

Many thanks to Saleh Altoma for his assistance with clarifying aspects of the original text and for his continued interest in this project. To David Baker, Ann Townsend, and Chris Green for their enthusiasm and careful attention to the sound and clarity of the translations. And to Issa Boullata for his insightful comments on the introduction.

Timely and generous grants from the Guggenheim Foundation and the National Endowment for the Arts were helpful in allowing me to devote time to the project.

Thanks to the editors of the following periodicals for publishing a number of the poems appearing in this volume:

5 A.M.: "Crawling Plant"
Agni: "The Porcupine"
Aljadid: "Martyrdom," "A Vision"
Another Chicago Magazine: "The Chalets Bar"
Artful Dodge: "For Jamal Jumaa"
Atlanta Review: from "Daily Chores"
Banipal: "The Ends of the African North," "L'Akhdar Ben Youssef and His Concerns," "House of Mirth," "Solitude," "Endings," "The New Baghdad," "America, America," "The Hermit," "Reception"
The Blue Moon Review: "Thank You Imru ul-Qais," "Shatt al Arab"
Chattahoochee Review: "The Other Person," "Spanish Plaza," "A Secret," "Three Stories from Kuwait," "Whims," "The River"
Chelsea: "April Stork," "The Lost Letter"
Cider Press Review: "Summer"
Commonweal: "Sparrows"
Connecticut Review: "Inheritance," "Autumn," "The Cold"
Crab Orchard Review: "First Snow," "Nocturnal," "Old Pictures from Kout al-Zain"

Graffiti Rag: "Maryam Comes"

Indiana Review: "The Spring"

International Quarterly: "The Mouse," "Night in Hamdan," "A Naive Song to a Wounded Smuggler"

Iowa Review: "Happiness"

Jusoor: "A Friendship," "Tower," "1989," "Trying to Flee," "Night Fugitive," "In Their Hands," "To Socialism," "The Murdered Come Out at Night," "In Those Days," "Days of June"

The Kenyon Review: "Noontime," "The Collapse of the Two-Rivers Hotel"

The Literary Review: "The Attempt"

Meridian: "On L'Akhdar Again," "Oleander Tree"

Modern Poetry in Translation: "Algerian Glances," "Three Bridges," "How L'Akhdar Ben Youssef Wrote His Last Poem," "Enemies," "Poetry," "The Trees of Ithaca"

Paintbrush: "Solos on the Oud"

The Paris Review: "Attention"

Prism International: "About That Lizard, About This Night," "The Village"

Quarterly West: "Cavafy's House," "A Hot Night"

Rattapallax: "Lines," "A Cloud," "Scene"

River City: "The Forests"

River Styx: "Snow May Fall"

Spoon River Poetry: "Abduction," "The Kurdish Quarter," "Chemical Weapon"

Third Coast: "The Flags," "The Gardener," "The Moment"

Willow Springs: "On the Red Sea," "Insistence"

"Attention" and "Night in Hamdan" appeared in *The Space between Our Footsteps: Poems and Paintings from the Middle East,* Naomi Shihab Nye, editor, published by Simon & Schuster, 1998.

"America, America," "The Hermit," and "Reception" appeared in *A Crack in the Wall: New Arab Poetry,* Margaret Obank and Samuel Shimon, editors, published by I. B. Tauris & Co., Ltd., 2001.

CONTENTS

Damascus/Amman (1992-1997)

INTRODUCTION

Most critics of modern Arabic literature would agree that Arabic poetry underwent more formal experimentation and linguistic and thematic shifts this century than in all of its rich history put together. As a new century begins, Saadi Youssef stands as one of modern Arabic poetry's seminal practitioners. Beginning in the 1950s, and now comprising about forty volumes of poetry, numerous works of translation, memoir, criticism, and fiction, Saadi's output is an impressive component of modern Arabic literature. His high status is in some way in contrast to the subtlety of his works, some of which are collected in volumes aptly titled *Ughniyat Laysat lil-Akharin* (*Songs Not for Others*, 1955) and *Qassa'id Aqalu Samtan* (*More Silent Poems*, 1980).

What surrounds Saadi Youssef's poetry is not stardom or controversy, as he never claimed to speak for anyone, even as he addressed the most public of concerns. Among readers, critics, and a generation of younger poets who have found in him their most influential model, Youssef's career is surrounded by an aura of gratitude and admiration for his commitment to poetry in the pursuit for social justice and individual liberty. Youssef's greatest contribution to contemporary Arabic poetry lies in his consistent effort to preserve the dignity of personal experience, despite and within a context of difficult sociopolitical realities in his native Iraq and in the Arab world at large.

Writing in a country and within a larger national postcolonial culture torn between powerful and power-hungry ideological currents, Youssef's reclamation of lived experience and defense of individual integrity make him one of the most important Arab poets today. His insistence on his private voice, on evolving his subjectivity through poetry, has been a great risk. After wrestling with stagnant traditions and the forces of colonialism, the creation of personal freedom was the third frontier for Arab poetry. In traversing this space, Youssef stands as a true pioneer, and that has been his lasting influence.

Throughout his years of exile and in the various places he lived and traveled, Youssef — like the Greek poet Yannis Ritsos, who was an important influence — wrote daily, positioning the writing of poetry as his emotional and spiritual home. The poems look out to the world, yet they are spoken from the awareness of the poet's calling and possess a sense of personal centrality, even as the outside seems intent on shattering the individual who has to keep moving. The poems contain dates and often their places of composition. In doing so, Youssef reclaims himself — his past, his present condition, his readings, and his previous writings — as the center, fleeting and illusive as it may seem, from which his poetry comes.

Saadi Youssef was born in the village of Abulkhasib near Basra, Iraq, in 1934. He completed his primary education there and received a degree in Arabic from the Teachers' College at Baghdad University in 1954. Demonstrating socialist sympathies early on, his first experience with exile was instigated by an unauthorized trip to a youth conference in Moscow in 1957 — forcing him to settle in Kuwait until the 1958 revolution in Iraq. In the 1960s, after a stint in jail, Youssef moved to newly independent Algeria, where he taught high school and worked in journalism. He returned to Iraq in 1971 to work in the Ministry of Culture but left for good in 1979, the year Saddam Hussein assumed power. Since then, Youssef has lived in Syria, Lebanon, Tunisia, Yemen, Cyprus, Yugoslavia, France, Jordan, and England, working mainly in journalism and in publishing. Youssef, also an important translator into Arabic, has published renditions of Walt Whitman, Constantine Cavafy, Yannis Ritsos, and Federico García Lorca, as well as novels by Ngugi wa Thiongo, Wole Soyinka, and David Malouf, among many others. During the 1990s, he lived between Amman and Damascus, where he edited the journal *Al-Madaa* before his recent relocation to London.

Saadi Youssef started writing while in his teens in the 1950s, just as Arabic poetry was breaking away from its most rigid formal aspect, the two-hemistich, rhymed line. His first volume, written in the traditional form, a book-length poem titled *Al-Qursan (The Pirate),* was published in 1952. His second volume, the aforementioned *Ughniyat Laysat lil-Akharin (Songs Not for Others)*, contained poems that made full use of the innovations advanced by Iraqi poets Badr Shakir al-Sayyab and Nazik al-Malaika with the new *taf'ila* (free verse) form. In this new development, the poet disregarded the traditional rules of Arabic prosody by employing the single metrical foot as the rhythmic unit instead of a set number of feet, and he eliminated rhymes or used irregular ones. The *taf'ila* also allowed the poet to write lines of various length, emphasizing a more personal rhythm. Youssef made a great deal of use of his newly given freedom. His rhyming skills were impeccable, and the modernist associative shifts in his poems demonstrated that the poet, not the form, was in charge.

More than any of his contemporaries, Youssef realized that the new flexibility widened the ranges a poem can traverse. The *taf'ila* poem, in Youssef's formulation, worked through a tension of associative expansion and musical contraction. In this regard, his use of repetition is central to understanding the balance he strikes between regularity and improvisation. In the traditional two-hemistich form, the single rhyme formed an organic unifier of the poem, even as the poet moved from one topic to another. Ultimately, the monorhyme — and this is part of the reason it failed to satisfy the young modern poets — seemed artificial and incapable of creating compositional unity on its own. For Youssef, repetition of certain lines created the symmetry that modern poetic unity demanded and allowed him to widen the scope of the poem. Open-ended and inconclusive as his poems may seem, they nonetheless leave us with an echoing impression of familiarity with their subject matter

·····

Youssef has suffered the travails that characterize the life of the Arab postcolonial intellectual and artist, an unholy trinity of political defeat, persecution, and exile. "A life of forced departures," as he says. In the late 1970s, isolated under the newly established dictatorship of Saddam Hussein and working in the Iraqi Ministry of Culture, Youssef began to receive a train of visitors. First came acquaintances from artistic and intellectual circles inviting him to join the Baath party, the country's governing body. When these efforts failed to convince him, he was transferred from a director in the Ministry to an assistant manager of a government library in an agricultural district. The visitors, connected with this branch or this department of the party, continued to come, at home and at work. Finally, the last of them warned him, "We give you ten days to join. We are a party 'branch'; the next people who will contact you will come from the security forces." Youssef's contacts to remedy his situation went nowhere. Friends became unavailable, people hung up the phone. Youssef decided to leave the country before being placed on the security-forces list. His last gesture: he boarded a train to Abulkhasib, his village near Basra, sat at a popular tea house, and took a last look at the streets and the faces.

In August 1982, Youssef left Beirut with Palestinian fighters at the end of the Israeli invasion of Lebanon. He had been writing for Palestinian publications and insisted on staying put during the vicious Israeli bombardment. As the poem "Maryam Comes" informs, Youssef was actively reporting on the Palestinian fighters, keeping abreast of the events around him at great personal risk. He left Beirut with the fighters, under an assumed name, wearing military fatigues and handing in a borrowed gun as his ticket onto the ship departing for Tartous.

In January 1986, Youssef was forced to leave socialist South Yemen when a coup attempt turned into a bloody civil war. South Yemen was a genuine respite for Youssef, a place where he felt at home. He was particularly proud of his achievements there, working as a cultural consultant, establishing a publishing house, publishing the country's first children's magazine and its first weekly magazine, where he wrote a regular column. After his home was bombed, as electricity and water were cut, he and others took refuge in a school. People dug a well in the school, the poet reports in one of his essays, and when it ran dry, dug another and another to remain alive. Soon the newly built school became a target of insurgent artillery, its walls collapsing on the people taking shelter in it. The hotel he fled to had bodies laid out in its lobby. The airport halls and runway were thronged with crows feeding on the remains of a massacre.

In France after the Gulf War in 1991, the poet helped form an Iraqi society in Paris, a club of Iraqi expatriates and exiles. The French

Interior Ministry soon contacted Youssef, who was the organization's elected president. The official informed him that the Ministry had full reports on the society's meetings and had some, but insufficient, information regarding its activities and aims. The official then asked if Youssef would help with information on the organization and its members:

— "We would like you to collaborate," said the official.
— "Sir, I don't like that word," Youssef replied.
— "What word?" asked the official.
— "Collaborate!" replied the poet.

"It was then that I had to leave Paris," writes Youssef, "unwillingly, again."

What's striking about Youssef's career is that the departures did not impede his artistic practice or shake his political commitment. The failure of the masses to join his socialist cause, a fact he sensed early on, did not diminish his desire to play an important role through writing, through poetry in particular. In a 1992 acceptance speech of a literary prize, he wrote:

> I remember, once, my detention: I was taken from home to the police station. After passing nights there, a policeman led me handcuffed to the train station — the train was going up from Basra to Baghdad, where I would be tried. We — the policeman and I — were on foot. The road between the police station and the train station passed by the places I knew and where I am known: the souk, the cafés, the bookstore. People were stirring in their daily bustle, and I was walking hand-cuffed among them. No one said to me, "Peace be upon you." No eyes batted for me. The people were preoccupied with their own affairs, which had nothing to do with me.
>
> O for the dreary endeavor!
>
> But at the last turn towards the train station, I saw a lad whose eyes whispered to me that he would tell the town my story. Of this lad I wrote. The artist discovers his beacon and raises his mountain where the flame blazes.

The absence of disappointment is remarkable. The investment in hope sparked by the imagination is a sign of spiritual resourcefulness and indefatigability. What Youssef gathered from that experience and the fact that he remains true to that harvest attest to the ongoing and enriching gift of poetry, both to the poet and to the reader of poetry.

The observations noted above describe Youssef's ambition for poetry. But what can it offer us? And who is it for? These questions have presented a persistent challenge to Arabic poetry throughout this century. An important phase of modernizing Arabic poetry in the first decades of the twentieth century was characterized by vicious and relentless attacks on occasional verse that addressed public events, issues, and personalities. A romantic phase won the battle and dominated by the 1930s, generating poetry that addressed suppressed personal feelings and almost ignored public concerns altogether. Mid-century, the emergence of newly independent and largely dictatorial Arab states, neocolonialism, and the loss of Palestine to Zionism brought to poetry, and literature at large, new challenges and issues to confront. Ideas on committed writing as well as the concept of socialist realism excited many aspiring writers and were the catalyst of numerous literary careers. These borrowed notions, reformulated in local terms, coalesced with the Arabic poetic tradition that posited the poet as a spokesman for his people. Modern Arabic poetry, or *al-shi'r al-hadith*, with al-Sayyab, al-Mala'ika, and others empowered with innovative formal techniques, offered a new type of verse that attempted to fuse individual aspirations and public national aims. Al-Sayyab's poem *"Unshudat al-Mattar"* ("Rain Song"), considered the quintessential early modern poem, begins with a love dirge describing the beloved's eyes and opens up into a discourse on poverty and the struggle of the masses in Iraq. After *"Unshudat al-Mattar,"* purely romantic poetry lacking perspective on the social reality surrounding it seemed hollow; purely nationalist writing seemed to ring false with its overtones of paternalism and impersonality. For Youssef, the association with al-Sayyab, with whom he shared his early work, still resonates with their shared social concern and commitment to experimentation.

While Youssef affirms that his Marxist orientation is a "guide in dealing with phenomena," he is by no means an ideologue. "The social and political concept ought to remain latent in the text, absorbed by the artist's blood. They should not float on the surface, so as not to disturb the structure of the artistic work," he explains. Poetry can only be an exploration of ideology, not a means of expressing belief in it. Reluctant to declare his ideology as the way out of alienation, Youssef shows how his ideology, transmuted within poetry, generates feelings of empathy and solidarity. For Youssef then, the commitment to justice and freedom stand beside his poetry, not above it. His political values, manifested in active participation in social struggle, are in reality fulfilling his abiding devotion to beauty. Justice and compassion in Youssef's verse are presented in a sensual manner that symbolizes his individualized appreciation of harmony and balance. They are aesthetic choices first and foremost.

Critics have noted that Youssef prefers whispering to declaiming. The metaphor of a whisper is appropriate as it captures both the intimacy and the urgency of an utterance. Neither a wholly controlled emotion, nor an expression of highly theoretical thoughts, a whisper is a short, intimate utterance that is half thought and half feeling. Between the polarities of abstraction and personal expression, Youssef seems to have developed a continuum of observation that precedes both. In a recent interview, Youssef stressed observation and description as a building platform of his poetic process:

> As a form of training . . . it is important that the poet develop
> a strong bond with life, to be able to observe and able to
> choose his subject matter. . . . Afterwards, he can abstract
> things by abstracting coincidences, and symbolize them. This
> time of observation (for a poet) is an elementary process akin
> to learning reading and writing.

His early poems rely heavily on observation in all its various manners: purely imagistic writing as in "Night in Hamdan," "Night Fugitive," and "The River"; personal portraits such as "Three Stories from Kuwait"; and dramatic monologues such as "Insistence" and "A Naive Song to a Wounded Smuggler." The poetry, primarily imagistic, is not impersonal, as the poet insists on his role as witness with phrases such as "I saw" or "I see now." The portraits are of people the speaker of the poem knows and cares for. In the poet's Algerian experience, a great deal of observational writing coalesced into the poems of L'Akhdar Ben Youssef, a persona who has served as the poet's double. By the 1970s, Youssef's observational continuum took its shaping and became a kind of poetic *modus operandi*.

As the poet continued to travel from one country to another, a pattern emerged: a series of short, imagistic poems where the poet assumes a neutral voice are then followed by a longer, much more complicated poem. "Enemies," one of Youssef's best poems, a three-movement work, brings together years of imagistic, observational writing embodied in his shorter poems. The poem partly relies on the reader's familiarity with Youssef's earlier works and his renditions of life by the Euphrates and the marshes of Shatt al Arab. "Enemies" brings these images and river narratives to a highly crafted level of concision through the use of montage. The narratives here are not catapulted by linear narration, but through elaboration on images. The blood in the water, the wild boar in the grass and its smell, the leader-warrior Abdelhassan Ben Mubarak, the circling shark, and the airplane hovering above are reworked and reformulated as poignant signifiers of terror, starvation, powerlessness, and unfulfilled hopes.

In this continuum, the seemingly neutral observations in the shorter poems are shot through a musical reconfiguration that combines both expression and abstraction, a meditation that is both cerebral and emotional. This complicated strategy, however, reflects the true processes of observation, where the observer stands between thinking and feeling, a perceptual intensity that is both calm and full of surprises. In "America, America," written in 1995 in response to hardships faced by the Iraqi people under U.S.-led sanctions, we experience the culmination of Youssef's experimentation with surprise and discovery.

Several critics have commented on the issue of surprise and suspension of closure in Youssef's poems. Youssef reports that he became fascinated with the idea early on in his career. This emphasis on the aesthetic and perceptual value of surprise saved his poetry from being overrun by his ideological affiliation. In the earlier poems, the word "suddenly" appears regularly in the shorter poems, usually given a line on its own to mark a shift in the poem, a new event, or a new realization. The surprise is marked in other poems by dotted lines that convey unwritten passages, a rupture in the sequential ordering of events, leading to shifts in the dramatic, or even musical, action of the poem. In the shorter, more ascetic poems written in the 1990s, such indications of a shift or a surprise are no longer given. Poems such as "On the Red Sea," "Attention," "The Cold," and "Happiness" are spare observations filled with suspense, riddle-like in their compactness.

This lyrical sensibility seems to be the cornerstone of Youssef's poetics in the later, longer poems "The Hermit" and "The Trees of Ithaca" and can even be witnessed in earlier works such as "How L'Akhdar Ben Youssef Wrote His Last Poem," written in 1976. Here we see a movement away from the earlier modes of portrayal and narration to an imagistic and syntactical intensity where the poet attempts to preserve the pleasures of the short lyric within the longer, more symphonic works. These layered poems develop epic resonance through their lyrical gaps. Youssef capitalizes on the essential component of the epic, that being, as Bowra noted, its lyrical digressions. These disconnected digressions preserve surprise as if the poet is making a mural out of a lyrical collage. Through these leaps in his scope of observation, we realize the epic nature of his vision. More than the pleasure of narration or portrayal, the poet informs us he's interested in the senses. He writes, "The senses are the aim of poetry's wave. They are the aim because they are its receivers. . . . And the idea is that the person's relation to the universe is returned to its earliest stages, to its spontaneity."

Youssef's emphasis on engaging the senses has an important ethical component. The tension between the title and the text proper in poems from "Insistence" and "Night Fugitive," written in the 1950s, to that of "For Jamal Jumaa" and "On the Red Sea," written in the 1990s, sends us tumbling into the dramatic situation. The absence of context and the foregrounding of details in these poems raise questions about the background of each of these dramatic situations. The reader becomes engaged in the politics by holding only a few precise details. Our experience of injustice, poverty, and tyranny is achieved through the awareness that we generate as readers. Youssef does not use his characters and narratives for the reader's cathartic benefit, but to create a sustained interest in his subject matter.

Ultimately, Youssef chooses to surprise and defamiliarize, rather than take an ironic stance. By unsettling our expectations, he is attempting to imbue the world with potential. His preference of the present tense over the past tense emphasizes this dynamism of the world. As in many of his observational poems, much of what is being depicted are not real events but imagined possibilities. Observing birds leaning on a stalk triggers the image of a thousand birds flying under the poet's shirt. And watching a cloudy sky in winter leads the poet to imagine a whole magical possibility of snow. In these short poems, the poet is suggesting a way of perceiving that aims at triggering within his readers a similar facility to go beyond immediate perceptions and beyond the past tense and the specter of irony it drags around with it.

Resistance to easy forms of irony is further demonstrated through resistance to closure and the use of dialogue. The poet prefers to repeat a line as a refrain or even a passage as a chorus, rather than provide a clincher. Repetition, often of the first lines of the poem at the end or throughout the poem, tends to unsettle linear readings. The refrain or the chorus creates musical anchors that allow the poet to range farther from his starting point, to digress, and to take risks. Not aiming to write ideas, rather to suggest them, Youssef provides the reader with meditations constructed through musical and imagistic associations.

Destabilizing the unity of the lyric voice further enhances the dynamism of association. Though the poet's basic composition is textual, many of the poems use such simple language as to seem orally based. Clearly, the use of repetition evokes the sonorities of orature, but Youssef is also aware of the poem's visual effect. The blank dotted lines, the deliberate shifts in line lengths, and indentations can only have effect when read, not when heard. The visual registers of thematic or tonal shifts are matched in other passages by the use of dialogic devices, voices that interrupt the established flow of the poem. In the poem "Whims," the poet metapoetically critiques his own lyrical sensibility. He asks himself, "Saadi, / my reasonable sir, / what are you writing tonight?" The poet leaves the struggle unresolved, suspending the poem between its tender vulnerability and its crusty self-deprecation. Similarly, in the poem "Insistence," the speaker's incessant pleading with Salim Marzouq to take him on his boat equally registers Marzouq's demand that the speaker sleep with him as a form of payment.

The L'Akhdar Ben Youssef poems represent an expansion of this dialogic approach. Developed in the late 1960s, the character of L'Akhdar shares many of Youssef's attributes: a poet, an exile, and a romantic admirer of taverns and their denizens. L'Akhdar is not merely a portrait, but a figure with whom the poet converses in, and seemingly out, of the poems. Concisely rendered, their differences and agreements are neutrally presented and fade away as if they are a conversation we barely overhear, but cannot seem to forget.

With the new "ascetic" poems, where Youssef abandons all formal constraints, we see the poet boldly and impatiently removing all strictures against his privacy. As the poet suggests in the poem "Poetry," writing is the place where the shards of the broken mirror, the dismembered world, are put together as the poet wishes. These are the moments when the poet is at his ethical and spiritual best. Youssef's private achievements embrace us and the tangible world we live in, making these poems more impressive than usual, more than poetry is supposed to be.

Upon taking a serious interest in Youssef's work in the early 1990s, I was struck by the staying power of his poetry. The individual poems, beautifully crafted as they were, seemed to work through accumulation. Few poets had made such an impression on me. Youssef's rich imagery and the subtlety and depth of his empathy were a contrast to the rhetorical loudness and political concentration that much of modern Arabic poetry wore proudly on its sleeve. I was charmed by "The Mouse." "Night in Hamdan" with these striking lines made a lasting impression on me:

> This is Hamdan . . .
>   tuberculosis and date palms.
> In Hamdan we hear only what we say,
> our night, the date palms, esparto grass,
> and the old river
> where lemon leaves on the water drift.
> They are green like water
> like your eyes, I say.

With so much movement and dynamism within a few lines, the horror of tuberculosis stands only a few words from an expression of love. Hamdan's provinciality and poverty stand in utter contrast to the natural beauty of the area and the poet's love for it. The transition from seemingly neutral description to a direct address confirms that the depiction is not without passion. Beside the musical rhythm of this passage, the shifts in the point of view establish a perceptual rhythm as well. Youssef allows us to assemble our own impressions and generate our own emotional reactions in the first few lines. But the poem is also an opportunity to express feelings that the reader can only acknowledge and not experience directly. Yet it is our participation in perceiving the poem in the seemingly neutral descriptions that establishes the intimacy of the poem and makes the last lines even more poignant.

This level of complexity achieved through very simple language was alluring. It kept me reading and looking for more of the poet's work. As a native speaker of Arabic whose primary language is English, I find that my appreciation of Arabic poetry is mediated by instant, even unconscious translation. Rendering Youssef's poems to English came naturally. But like the act of reading these poems, where a single one is insufficient, even the simplest of Youssef's poems took much revising to render satisfactorily. I continued to translate as I read more of the poet's work; yet much as I liked many of his poems, I was aware early on that his corpus is too large to gather in a collected volume. It would take a lifetime of translation to bring all of his works into another language.

In choosing the poems, it seemed appropriate to learn the poet's own writing process. The size of Youssef's body of work, for instance, indicates the experimental approach he takes to writing. His prolific production suggests that not every attempt he made was going to succeed. Some days were a gift to him and he wrote several excellent short poems in a row. Those intense days are represented here. In the spirit of the poet's own process, most of the translations were sparked by the creation of an interesting phrase. If a poem didn't invite that creativity, I left it for another reading.

Translating these poems, I felt that I needed to develop a critical assessment of Youssef's work to guide my selection process. Reading criticism of the poet's work was essential for this collection to take into account the poet's career and stylistic and thematic changes. Some poems opened up years after repeated readings. In some cases, I was aided by grasping the musical structure; in other cases, critical analysis made the translation possible.

A career as large as Youssef's had to be reflected through a large selection that takes into account his formal and thematic shifts. Dividing this volume according to the poet's numerous collections would have chopped it into small and seemingly artificial divisions. Furthermore, these shifts didn't seem to be reflected as dramatically in his volumes as they were in his transitions from one place to another. Youssef admits to being "a poet of place," one who cannot write without taking stock of his surroundings. Towards the second half of his career, this geographical orientation became more evident. The Beirut poems in the early 1980s were titled as such. The Algeria and Yemen poems of the same approximate period were also selected in separate volumes. *Qassaid Paris (The Paris Poems)* served as the subtitle of his book *Ashjar Ithaka (The Trees of Ithaca)*, published in 1992. A volume published in the late 1980s containing poems that were written in various places was titled *Muhawalat (Attempts)*, accurately reflecting the poet's sense of geographical and even technical displacement. The Damascus/Amman period, starting in the early 1990s, suggests the poet's preference for the short, compact lyric that has been his mode since then. Of all the poet's collections, only the first book, *Al-Qursan (The Pirate)*, is not represented here.

Finally, these translations were aided by the poet's cooperation. He proved to be as personable as his poetry. A prompt correspondent, he replied quickly to questions and provided incisive answers. Some led to revisions of lines or passages; others were incorporated as notes. Asked to suggest poems that he would like to see represented, Youssef repeatedly left the choice up to me. Translation, he suggested, is a kind of authorship. It cannot be done without freedom and individual inspiration. Youssef's career attests to the discipline and persistence inspiration requires from the poet; concerted efforts in patient silence are poetry's austere and lonely labors.

K. M.

WITHOUT AN ALPHABET, WITHOUT A FACE

RECEPTION

Snow falls on the cacti, then a cry and a café, a star and encampments, a priest's gown ripped by wolves, shoes made of fine leather. How do turtles shiver on the shores of Hadramaut? The full moon moans from the bottom of the river . . . and the girls scream in rapture. I do not need a bullet. My only fortune in this world is the wall behind my back. How green the grass on the steppes of Shahrazour! I saw a rope dangled. Where is Youssef? I was in the markets of Timbuktu . . . and I labored. One night a ship sailed us through the shoals of Djibouti. . . .

Mogadishu tosses lamb meat to the sharks. I have no destination. I have a cat that has begun lately to tell me the story of my life. Eternity ever coming nearer, why have you too betrayed me? This afternoon I will learn to sip the brutality of flowers. What does treachery taste like? Once I traveled, taken by my song? The soldiers' trains roll on. . . . Rolling. Roll on. Rolling. Roll on. Rolling. . . . The snow of Moscow warms my tears. There is no virtue to herdsmen when they settle and when they set for travel. . . . Cities dissolve villages with the shake of a finger. My bread is made of coarse rice flour, and the salt on my fish is ash. There is no chance I will be her lover tonight in the girls' dormitory. No. . . . On Saturdays she closes her door to me. I will burn the papers. The inspector may arrive. On the night train I dozed off in my chains. And the wooden seat was my plane that crashed. They are chanting for you, girl of the harbor tavern. The strangers returned from their search for diamonds. On the stone of Hejja the eagles of Hemiar take their rest. Once I almost found the child-moon in my palm. Why did the people leave the park? I do not want your hand. Do not toss me your rope made of tatters. Today I have found another torrent:

Welcome Life. . . . Welcome my other lover.

Amman, 23/3/1997

Basra / Kuwait / Baghdad
1955–1963

NIGHT IN HAMDAN

We in Hamdan say:
Sleep when the date palms sleep.
When the stars rise over Hamdan
the lights of the huts are put out,
the mosque and the old house.
It is the long sleep
under the whispers of faded palm fronds:
the long death.
This is Hamdan . . .
     tuberculosis and date palms.
In Hamdan we hear only what we say,
our night, the date palms, esparto grass,
and the old river
where lemon leaves on the water drift.
They are green like water
like your eyes, I say.
You, in whose eyes I behold spring,
how can a friend forget you?
I will meet you
when the setting of the stars covers Hamdan
when night bears down on the city.
. . . .
. . . .

Together we will roam the depths of Baghdad
when the setting of the stars covers Hamdan.

Basra, 1955

INSISTENCE

Salim Marzouq, take me   on a ship
on a ship. Take my eyes for ransom. . . . I'll do what you wish
except what women are supposed to.
Salim Marzouq   my sad wife
is a prisoner in her father's house
in a village near Sihan, arid without palms.
Her father moans from want
like a cat in cold winter.
Salim Marzouq   I'll do as you wish
except what women are supposed to.
Salim Marzouq   father of goodness
if I don't go, she'll choke from weeping.
She'll die in the cold of winter
from her father's stinginess and the night of winter.
Salim Marzouq

                        she's not like other women.
She's sweet, Salim Marzouq   Weeping wilts her.
She's a child and the moon still cheers her.
And she fears the pouring rains of winter.

Ah, Salim Marzouq. . .

Basra, 1956

NIGHT FUGITIVE

Everything rises now from the drowned past
on this night in May
                              with a candle, wind,
two books, and an old pair of trousers.
This is how it is:
the candle shakes
lightly
and the shade of the date palms turns green.
A ship on the river
nears land little by little.
This is how it is.
The stars sent blue flickers
like your eyes.
It is the turbulence in the depth of sorrow.
This night in May will pass, my friend
with two books and an old pair of trousers.
Will you return safely one day,
a dove on your shoulder?
. . . .
. . . .
. . . .

Everything rises now from the drowned past.
It has been two years
and he has not returned.
One day the child will throw his arms around us.
He will come with two books
and a new pair of trousers.
He will always return safe.

Basra, 1956

IN THEIR HANDS

And when you're thrown from your room
startled, and your ribs bruised
blue like the dead
on a black night
                        murdered,
think of Basra,
think of what we love
and what we sing of from the heart:
sun, bread, and love.
. . . .
Think with Basra.

Basra, 1956

A NAIVE SONG TO A WOUNDED SMUGGLER

Night horseman, my house is here,
my house by the river.
Stop by once
and leave a tender dream in my heart.
I am alone behind the door.
And night. . . . Oh how long it lasts!
If strangers knew
that I stand behind the door,
no nightingale would serenade the stream.
Stop by our place, tender young man.
Twenty rivers flooded.
They were covered with roses and fish
covered with reddened leaves.
Here is the crossing.
Come by our road,
O tender hope.
In the grass I hear
tired green hooves
drenched in dew.
And you — did you know
that I am behind the door
in a transparent dress?
And my mood is tender.
Night without darkness
as if veiled by a star
and my horseman is soiled with mulberries,
his face a star
lighting my heart with tender gladness.
I am alone behind the door

and my horseman is coming, coming.
But he's sleepy.
Smeared with mulberries and silence,
he doesn't even glance at my door.

Basra, 1957

MARTYRDOM

A steel spear in the belly of Jesus. . . .
It rips him and drags him for hours
like a cotton flower soaked in blood.
After Jesus, death leaves in its wake
a blood moon, and a stumbling evening
filthy and long.
The spear digs a path in the softness of flesh
and hammers with steel a relentless heart
into the heart of Jesus.
Here his severed head rolls off,
ninety daggers in his throat.
. . . .
. . . .
The informants rush away,
tripping on the head of Jesus.
And in the print shops the filthy newspapers
drink his blood between their coughs,
black, contemptuous, and prolific.

Basra, 1957

THE MOUSE

Here you are alone again
as though you had never traveled
through everyone's earth.
Here you are alone like a bird
tossed by the north winds to Kuwait.
Is this what you wished?
        To be alone
turning your eyes, waiting for the mail
as if the pages of the letters were waves
that would carry
your tired heart away.
And slowly in the darkness of the sea
        you will see her hands
waving among flowers,
light filling her eyes.
Return!
Return to yourself, you tramp,
you who roam without a house.
Return to yourself; damn the poets. You are in Kuwait
like a mouse looking for a job,
looking for white cheese to eat.
Leave that girl alone.
And when you fill your stomach tomorrow,
send her a thousand songs.

Kuwait, 1/10/1957

TO SOCIALISM

On the snow
winter wrapped its coat around itself.
The winds were mad,
their gales shaking
as if wounded by the cold air.
And there
on the course of their ship
was my heart
and Petersburg
and wind.
I open my heart to sunlight.
I will forgo it for your earthly face.
O seed,
when your planter is ready to sow,
you burst out of his songs.

8/6/1958

A SECRET

At noon you stand by her room . . .
your hands turn to stone
instantly.
You stand by the door. Take a step
and enter:
        her pillow there,
her books . . . her silver belt discarded,
the remains of her perfume, a newspaper
embracing the floor.
The curtains are not velvet.
And
her bed, frozen in silence, is asking
about her lowered eyelids.
You think: If only she were here,
if only you could close your eyes
on a night with her
in the silence of her room,
her fingers dozing here,
her tresses lying there,
and you beside her
dreaming of a brook . . .
. . . .
And now that you've scandalized
the secrets of her room:
Aren't you ashamed?

Baghdad, 30/4/1960

THE MURDERED COME OUT AT NIGHT

At night they awake,
their white eyes forever open wide.
And in the city, even through its narrow alleys,
they walk, their shrouds hardly concealing their limbs.
They walk. Their mouths are orchards
of lead, singing, and the alleys resound.

We hear them when the children shiver.
No other sound can voice this wild despair.
A sound that knocks on doors and burns
like a bird crossing the valley of death and flowering.
May ends . . . and from the waves of its banners
blood will gush to startle a dozing nation.

Baghdad, 2/9/1960

WHIMS

1.

He wanted to stop her once
in the middle of a busy street
to ask her, to slap her, or to offer
himself to shield
her wondrous forehead.
But she walked on, and the fire remained
lost in his heart . . .

2.

If word had come from her,
his world would have rained
apple blossoms
and his eyes would have closed.
O word he loves,
O single word.
All my life is a single word.
O single hope.

3.

She was told he had arrived;
a smile passed on her lips.
She waited two days,
waited two months —
knitting —
until that star disappeared.

4.
I laugh at what I write today.
I say: "Saadi,
my reasonable sir,
what are you writing tonight?"

Basra, 15/3/1961, 1:20 A.M.

THREE STORIES FROM KUWAIT

Hamoud's Death

They didn't dig a grave for him
in the bleakness of the desert
in its eternal sand and muted screams.
They didn't wet his lips before his death.
They didn't hear his words of sand.
They could not
dig a grave for him or wipe his lips
or listen to his sayings.
All are dead like him
in the bleakness of the desert.

Abu Dahab

He was a shy smuggler with coal eyelashes,
a silk kaffiyeh draped on his shoulder.
At night he sang about lovers
and the flame of yearning
and a date palm in a courtyard
where lovers wept.

When we returned years ago from exile in Kuwait
he told me about his love, a sweet one at home.
Then he shut his eyelashes — shyly —
          and a breeze passed over the water.

Abu Dahab,
not a smuggler, even though he remained
shy, his eyelashes coal,
a silk kaffiyeh draped on his shoulder.
Abu Dahab,
the story of travelers and mail.
Safwan to Matlaa! or *Matlaa to Safwan!*

Yesterday in the humidity of Basra and her marshes
I asked him about the travelers and the mail.
But he was a shy smuggler with coal eyelashes,
a silk kaffiyeh draped on his shoulder,
and he was troubled,
a stranger,
his lids heavy on his eyes.

Abdallah Samarah
He was from Jordan. The world threw him with me
in a cursed village that hates to live.
He loved white cheese and olives,
tart zaatar
and lemons
and the name of the one he loved
and a flag fluttering in the darkness of Jordan.

O if only he would pass by our home,
if only my hand could shake his again,
if only I could see the silence in his eyes,
if he would visit again to talk of his life's joys,
white cheese and olives,
lemons and tart zaatar
and the name of the one he loves and who loves him.

News of Abdallah:
in jail, or in the darkness of Jordan.

Baghdad, 3/8/1961

THE RIVER

A pathway of willows, water moss, and greenery
cuts through a sea of date palms.
A flower in my hat.
A river of basil,
silence and pomegranates
stretch to her shuttered home,
to rose shrubs in her orchard
and an insomniac moon
and sadness sailing its boat.

　　　　～

River, silver is swaying
　　　　　　on your green waters. Do not drown it.
From its basket, dawn is tossing
　　　　　　sunlight in radiant clusters of dew
like a frond with leaves of coral.

River, if you reach her house
to caress it, or to make it one of your banks,
take this flower to her,
take this coral flower to her.

Maybe with it
she will forget to forget.

　　　Basra, 28/1/1962

OLD PICTURES FROM KOUT AL-ZAIN

My Grandfather's Friend
When I met him, blue fog was rising from the date palms.
He was in his orchard feeding a bird in a cage
(fearing our cat; she gives the poor man no comfort).
Butterflies in his beard, roses, and shreds of pollen,
and like the god of grass, meadows stretched in his eyes;
water and flowers fluttered in springs of glitter.
Ah, red kaffiyeh drowning in greenness!
Night dew on your fringe, unravelings of cotton,
the gloss of mother-of-pearl, iris and damascene rose,
how long I wished
your ruby crown would once adorn my head!

The Cemetery
When night tumbles, the cemetery moans
and the djinn and the dead palms shake lifeless branches.
When the wind blares, a star yellows and falls.
A rain of yellow leaves waters the cemetery.

Mother of Lead
You, mystery of rivers, and taste of islands
in seas of palms, wrapped in sadness, tired, broken.
You, unknown, with your muddied beaches and black livelihood.
You, roads that no god has traveled to feed the living and the dead
or water their dreams with manna and quails.
Who, I wonder, will lift from your green curtains
the drowned secrets of your nights
as your dead drink the waters
of river stars?
        Do you know what the skulls hide
in the mud of their tombs?

Mother of lead,
when your dead drink the waters
of river stars, a ship will come to you
without anchor or sailors.
It will come like a raft
and the dead will open their mother-of-pearl eyes
and tread your black boards as the night halves —
carrying tea, perfumes, and soap
and weeping to no end.
On your black shores stars will shiver.
Dawn will pass over the palms
and women will ache with yearning
and dew will glitter
and the dead will return,
weeping over the ship
and the mud tombs that collapse,
waiting for nightfall . . .

Basra, 21/6/1962

DROWSINESS

In the wound of my silence, no wind blows,
no desert weeps,
no branch withers.
        Your eyes remain my riches and my home,
and the earthly world is flung on the floor, heavy-footed, and silent.
Like the sea I offer it waiting.
Like the sea it offers me shells.
But it is different from me —
only a thing where salt dissolves
the way a dream dissolves inside of me.
Two postcards without postage:
I etched their words on the walls of a cave
so they may sail the sea
and travel through thought, time and death.
So they may cross deserts
to report back to me in my garden
about a rose that lives in Bukhara.
So they may build me a home in the deserts of misery,
a palace with stars pummeling its seventy terraces,
and in its wide courtyards scorpion-sting thorns float.
There, owls and snakes will come for shelter
and the man who loves Bukhara.

                    ~

In the silence of my wound, you shiver
        your face like the stars, like pale sand.
On your crystalline neck a tattoo my lips made,
and your furrowed brow is stung by the stars.
Heaven, clear-watered heaven in my paper home,
what can the stars tell me when your luminous face is dim?
In the wound of my silence, again, the wind blows, deserts wail,
a branch withers and the sea turns the deserts blue.
Behind the palace of loss your eyes

weep over a song and a home
as if the earthly world is plotting its own end,
as if I am dying alone.

Don't wake me . . .
                            kiss me once again . . .
                                                    and sleep . . .

1963

Algeria
1964–1971

ALGERIAN GLANCES

The café facing the sea —
boughs stretch into it,
whispering to the five empty tables
in vain.
A woman weeps
alone
in summer dusk,
and the sea that listens
and the empty café.

~

Above the workers' blue shirts,
above the children's eyes   the dancer's   the sailor's,
above white houses   squares   flowers,
above the tears   euphoria   and trench,
a ship mast flutters through wind and marble
in a green horizon,
in a white horizon,
in a red horizon.

~

The pine hills give the drowsy moon
a window
with shutters made of boughs
and a balcony
to view the cloudy harbor
and its cloudlike sea.
A seagull descends
to its sleeping orchard
not followed by any eyes.

~

In a while the square will awaken.
Midnight buses will leave its stones and trees,
will leave it like an oasis.
In a while the square will hear
lovers' last whispers
and the guard's first words to the horizon.
In a short while this square will hear poetry.

Algiers, 21/7/1964

THE OTHER PERSON

For Lawrence Durrell

In a restaurant in winter, I heard him cough,
watched him wipe his hands with a handkerchief
and muffle a laugh in the depth of his eyes.
I watched him notice me for the first time,
mocking me without letting me hear a vowel,
or even stirring the silence that dozed.
The windows of the winter restaurant were wet.
Then suddenly, he left,
wrapped in his pale coat.

We met in train stations, drank tea with mint,
didn't talk. Horizons moved on, hour by hour,
and he seemed weighed by my company
and my quiet face. In Tlailat
he called out to me, but his cry was lost.
So he returned to his world in search of meaning,
watching me like a thief from the corner of his right eye.
Once again we parted
without saying: "To your health!"

Yesterday in my room with its shuttered windows,
I was singing, smiling to the soft rain and wind
and the flowers that were still
sleeping.
Then suddenly,
I heard a rap at the window.
Are the hands of the wind calling on me,
visiting me,
or does the lemon branch
want to come inside, fearing the wind?
Or is it a song of soft rain

31

coming from the ends of the earth to bring me
the scent of my overcast country?

I saw his wet eyes
through the misty glass.
And in them
I saw two songs.

Sidi-bel-Abbès, 25/11/1964

SPANISH PLAZA

O how many ships there are in Malaga . . .
and how bitter the cold in the square!
FEDERICO GARCÍA LORCA

The scent of a guitar in the square.
Tobacco and tourists in the café. . . .
              We were here yesterday.
I danced until my socks tore,
until I myself was torn.
. . . .

And her gravelly laugh disappears,
her dress fading in the corner of the square.

        ~

I left my keys in the sea.
I gave them to night and wind.
And when doors closed behind me,
I came to the square.

        ~

Gypsies of the tavern:
who will open the door to me?
The night horseman: who will wipe
the dust off his sleeves?
Who will remove summer dust and darkness
from the warm barrels?
Who will pick the olives, lemon trees and stars
behind his saddle?
Gypsies of the tavern:
the tavern is still closed
and the night horseman in his wandering
is asking about her promised door
and her abundant orchard.
Ten pimps follow him to the first house
on a dark street without a tavern to adorn it.

        ~

When Sinbad lifted the ice blocking the door,
when his hands shivered,
and as he sang waking the door's ten locks
and as he pushed in the door praying,
his eyes saw an eyeless snake sniffing at a flower.

⁓

Harbor Wharves, Harbor Wharves,
beginnings of the earth whose meeting I embrace,
ends of the earth whose sight I lost,
I have searched for her, never glimpsed her face
as if the only hands I shook were made of water
or black wine, or the blond drunkard's,
the bored musician's, the dancer's, or darkness.
Through thousands of cafés I almost found her,
and in a report about Alvarez's prison,
and in Alvarez's prison,
a secret behind night's shroud, plazas and noise,
behind the backs of the local police and tourists,
shoemakers and beggars.

⁓

Secret I entrusted to the wharves,
my hat flew with the wind
and on the water
a flower whirled.

Sidi-bel-Abbès / Malaga, 7/1/1965

THREE BRIDGES

You run alone, burdened
with bluish moss, forgotten and slow.
Waves glitter on you,
banks fall into you,
and in your abandoned silence
you carry them along with weeds
and carry them far away.
Your chest remains naked, dewed,
burdened with gifts
green like water, like dim mirrors,
a branch, a hat, a dead cat,
a child's shoe, a condom.
    The weeds braid ribbons around them,
and you, careful stepper, carry them
and bend them
                with your bending.
As days pass they become your water.
Waves glitter on them,
banks fall into them.
And you return again: gifts and mirrors.

First Bridge

I hid them under me.
    Night brought out its stars,
soaked them, washed them, and let them swim.
There were three; they held their stars,
but didn't wash them
              in water . . .
They waited.
    I felt the wheels crush my backbones.
The three hid behind the shadow of my chest
and I saw them running.
    Iron exploded and my back sank

in the water. The stars fell upon me then.
And the river ran
and night laid its golden white palms
on the ruins of my chest.

Second Bridge

The bridge leads to a small tree blossoming
with sparrows,
a princess listening out from her green balcony
for the sun's intimations.
There was a gate by her green waistline.
The river was a gate to her green waistline.
Princess:
          O how the bridge worships you!
It barely recognizes the river.
What is this water, this wayfarer passing by,
this visitor moving on?
And she barely recognizes the bridge.

Third Bridge

Lend me your hands.
Lend me your rough hands
and let me feel
your heartbeat against my arm.
Lend me your hand.
Let me feel the wind scream in the sail.
Lend me a hand for vigor, a glance toward a lost stream.
In the days when we saw the world
with a flame thin as a dream,
our black eyes shined on nothing
except on the veins on your arms,
shined on nothing except the steps of those

who pushed through their stone souls
lunging toward you.
Today, we lend you a hand to find our garden.
If only you would lend me your wounded hand,
O bridge-tomb!
Our black eyes are heavy lidded,
and my old boat is sailed by a blind captain.
But the garden remains the same.
Its red flowers have never seen
handkerchiefs waving good-bye.
Appointed hour in the midst of loss,
give me your rough hands to feel
your heartbeat against my arms.

Algiers, 1/4/1965

SOLOS ON THE OUD

1.

A clock rang for the tenth time,
it rang ten o'clock,
it rang ten.

Across from the church tower
a star flickered and disappeared
and a nightingale vanished in the pines
fading into a green mirage of night.
Come to my house, girl.
My house is my shrine.
My house is a shrine.
The church shut its doors
and the candles were put out
and the kerchiefs were stained with wine.

2.

On the park path
the water was silent, and the dry leaves
and the deep shadows.

On the park path
the sparrows didn't sing
and in the garden
the whispering brook didn't sing.

God of drowned alphabets,
where, where is the shiver of drowsy shadows?
Her hand is in mine
and in my chest a garden.

3.

Land where I no longer live,
distant land
where the sky weeps,
where the women weep,
where people only read the newspaper.

Country where I no longer live,
lonely country,
sand, date palms, and brook.
O wound and spike of wheat!
O anguish of long nights!

Country where I no longer live,
my outcast country,
from you I only gained a traveler's sails,
a banner ripped by daggers
and fugitive stars.

Algiers, 16/8/1965

OLEANDER TREE

In your light green clothes, you stand
abandoned to the corner of the square.
Trucks and shoes sprinkle you with dust
while the children in the square laugh.
They reach for your arms and their burned, bitter veins.
They plead with the tired guard: a flower.
"O Uncle Guard, can I take a flower?"
But your branches,
      children will not touch them.
They will not steal any of your flowers
because you're lost between the thing and its image.
Your names are lost,
lost like water.
Forgotten citadel, your locks are deserted.
Yet you stand stubborn between
carriage horses and black shoes,
raising your red flags in the square.

Algiers, 21/6/1967

SHATT AL ARAB

Dream 1.   On nights of torment and sorrow
        its waters saturate the pillow
        and it comes like the smell of moss
                    with green steps
        to touch my right palm
        with a jasmine sprig:
             Wake up. . . .
             I am the river. . . .
        Don't you love me? Don't you want to reach Basra
        on the wings of the pillow?
             River,
             I'm awake, awake.
                  "On my pillow a drop
                      that tastes like moss. . . ."
        It's Basra.

Dream 2.   Skies shade me.
        Low skies shade me and the sparrows,
        and my grandfather holds my hand,
        his face shaded with a red kaffiyeh.
        In the distance the waters shine
        and my grandfather holds my hand:
        "Let's go faster before the birds leave.
        Let's go faster before the tide robs our nets. . . ."

        On the grass, fish drip from our nets.
        In river fog they appear like green ships,

        like red ships,
        like blue ships
        that sailed before the water rose.

Dream 3.   On the shores of Kout al-Zain dawn was tumbling down.
The date palms wore purple plumes
and in my hair there were stars, warmth, and rain.
I was swimming toward the other bank,
swimming to reach Ahwaz.
And in Ahwaz dawn was tumbling down
and the date palms wore purple plumes
and the water in Karun tasted just like the water
in Basra.

Sidi-bel-Abbès, 4/5/1969

THE ENDS OF THE AFRICAN NORTH

On the sands of North Africa I carried palm fronds
and between the East and exile
I burned maps on Egyptian ports.
Through the alleys of Benghazi and Derna
I was asked about my identity card.
I'd torn it in two.
I gave the inspector a half
and the other to my beloved.

　　　﹏

In the neighborhoods of Tunis and their winter cafés
at the gates of Africa's spread thighs
I saw a girl weep
without an alphabet, without a face.
Snow was falling and a girl wept under it.

　　　﹏

Across distances you smile:
　　　and Morocco spun
in a recline of tangerine branches and rosy dreams of Seville.
Your missteps were there between shadow and darkness
and I saw you, alone, dreaming.
I watched a smile rise and color you with sunset,
nourishing the darkness with the hues of Rabat,
a rainbow-colored fountain square
　　　　　　　　from the evenings of Granada.

　　　﹏

Across distances you shiver.
　　　Morocco was spinning
like a record playing in the dark and you clung
to each minute. Morocco was spinning
and you clung to it,

you clung to its five-angled disc.
We were chained to its scents and the soft sands
of its beaches, weighed with white wine
until the sand slumber ended,
until the wine reddened, and the pictures blurred
and our lives were divided by the Bureaus of Aliens and Immigration.
Three months, and three, and three, and three more.

On the sands of North Africa I carried palm fronds.
I carried pollen from exile to exile.
The years were seven, and seven were the earths after you,
                    and seven the skies.

You're content here,
your faded fronds, your silenced water wheels and melted mud.
While you're here, little one,
my southern princess, do you forget your loved ones this easily?
Do you, southern city, accept the rot of exile
for someone who would die to see your face?

Besieged country, O tertiary face!
O hungry eyes gazing between stone and sea!
O nation of mirrors, O open wound, O tertiary root!
You're wounded, and we are your hemorrhage.
Yet we seek the wound and seek an opening to infinity.
Homeland besieged by those who fence their own eyes! O tertiary age!
You're a stranger,
        your face drawn like a sword,
                your eyes hungry for secrets.

You're a stranger in the earth that stretches
between the streams of Basra and the walls of Rabat.
I saw it branch by branch, stone by stone,

but labor pains are here in your eyes gazing
at mysteries and secrets,
at the carnations stuck in the mouths of rifles,
the waters, and the blue hues of Basra.

In central Morocco I saw your creased, limp hands
reach for me.
        They caressed my gray threads and disappeared.
And yesterday
        your lips visited me and whispered:
        "You're a young man again."

On the sands of North Africa I carried palm fronds
and a traveling pass.
Didn't you know that they withheld your passport once
and you slept on the street?
When you arrived snow was swirling
around the city's throat, and the trees
were cold glass made of water
and the spasming streetlights
spluttered the way snow splutters.
        Something touched the street
and stuck to it, frozen and slippery.
You will remember how once
they withheld your passport and you slept on the street?

In the markets of bel-Abbès,
in the city center,
in the cafés where coffee grains never settle in the bottom of the pot,
and in the bars where the hour is always late,
you will hear them whisper:
        "The emigrant has come."
        Then the hour is no longer late,

and a drop of beer becomes a thorn in my throat.
And in the Indian bazaar
and in my blood,
a clock will ring.

Why do the years wear lead shoes?
And will you die if you walked at night
behind the cypresses and the date palms,
behind the fluctuations of the weather and the newspapers,
behind the tourist hotels,
behind the unisex coats
and the quiet of the sand
until you met the sea,
until you disappeared with the sea,
until you were clothed in moss
in the drowsiness of the ocean floor
and the sailing ships?

Peace to the murdered.
Peace to the living.
Peace to you, partisan, soldier, and farmer.
Peace to workers.
Peace to you who walk on water.
Peace to the date palms that failed
to sate the children's hunger.
Peace to you, Land of Rifles
and Graves.
And to you, Circle of Life . . .
Peace.

Algiers, July / 1971

Baghdad
1972–1979

L'AKHDAR BEN YOUSSEF AND HIS CONCERNS

A prophet shares this apartment with me
and lives in my rectangular room.
Every morning he drinks coffee with me
and the secrets of long nights.
When he sits beside me,
and as he reaches for the cup
(on the French table made of glass and metal),
I see dark circles around his eyes.
In the wardrobe our clothes are the same:
he wears my shirt one day
and I wear his the other.
When he's angry
he refuses to wear anything except his woolen burnoose
and refuses me altogether.
He enters the fields
to plow
or to buy sugar
or to say his incantations.

When we met at a bar
he took a flower from his pocket and leaned toward me,
whispering that it's for me. "I brought it
across the Oujda walls where the borders are battlefields,
but" — he gave me the myrtle flower — "it's
yours now. Do with it what you wish,
but don't let me see it wilting in your pocket.
Ah Oujda, Oujda, the Skhairat Road
was blocked by the Royal Guards. I brought it
from there and hid it under my skin, the shoes
of the Royal Guards were heavy with nails."
He pointed to his chest quickly, then
closed his eyes. "Oujda, Oujda,
what will you look like if I see you again?"

He goes with me when I visit my beloved,
          enters ahead of me
and kisses her forehead.
He sits at the end of the dark room and stares long into her eyes.
When I sketch an unintelligible wish —
pillows or a house —
he begins to speak of an overflowing desire,
drawing eagles with chalk on the wall.
He comes closer to take the girl's hand (as I sit beside her)
and takes her out of the room.

At the Ceuta gate the customs officers sat at their desks,
drinking bad wine.
In the distance
the city celebrated the night of Eid:
fireworks piercing the tattered horizon
flashing
          flashing
                    flashing
and the customs officers remained at their desks,
chewing on bad wine.

She follows him shyly, their arms locked.
I wait at the intersection
and my girl laughs, pointing at storefronts.
He chides her and points instead at the rising trees.
They turn at the swimming-pool gate
and I quicken my pace behind them. There they are
entering the park. "Do you see the small branches?
Can you touch their budding greenery? Do you hear
the heartbeat throbbing in them? Bring that bough closer
to you. Let it touch your arms. Think
of yourself as its sap, let your forearm become

a canvas for it to draw its leaves, the freedom a child feels
when he touches his eyelids in the mirror."
Then he kisses my girl's hand.

I will use your name —
    pardon me —
                then your face.
You see how your face, on the second page,
is a mask for mine.
You see that I'm wearing the bloodred tie.
Do you remember it?
The day we were together in Husaima
where we bought it,
the day you went to the photographer
before the passport,
before traveling,
and I insisted you wear it.

The customs men were behind their desks,
chewing on bad wine,
the passport
staring at them, one by one,
at their stamps and their wine.

    Baghdad, 25/5/1972

IN THOSE DAYS

1.

On the first of May I entered Central Prison
and the Royal Officers registered me a communist.
I was tried, as was the custom then,
and my shirt was black with a yellow tie.
I left the hall followed by the soldiers'
blows and the derision of the judge. I had
a woman and a book of palm fronds. In it I read
the first names. I saw detention stations
filled with lice, others filled with sand,
others empty except of my face.
When we were thrown in the imprisonment that has yet to end,
I vowed: "This heart's yearning will not end."
You who will reach my kin, tell them it will not end.
Tonight we rest here, and in the morning we reach Baghdad.

2.

I celebrate this night with the moon visiting
from behind bars. The guard asleep, and the breathing
of Sibah is weighed with the humidity of the Shatt.
The visiting moon turns toward me. I am humming
in the corner of the holding station. What have you brought me
in your eyes? Air I can touch? Greetings from her?
The visiting moon enters through the bars and sits
on the corner of the station covered with my blanket.
He holds my palm. "You're lucky," he says
and leaves.
              And in my hands I held
                                a key made of silver.

All songs disappear except people's songs.
And if a voice can be bought, people will not buy it.
Willfully, I forget what is between people and me.
I am one of them, like them, and their voice retrieved.

   3.

On the third of May I saw six walls crack.
A man I knew emerged through them, wearing
workers' clothes and a black leather cap.
I said: "I thought you left. Wasn't
your name among the first on the list?
Did you not volunteer in Madrid? Did you
not fight along the revolution's ramparts in Petrograd?
Weren't you killed in the oil strike?
Did I not see you in a papyrus thicket
loading your machine gun? Did you not raise
the commune's red flag? Did you not organize
the people's army in Sumatra?
Take my hand; the six walls may collapse
at any moment. Take my hand."

Neighbor, I believe in the strange star.
Neighbor, life's nights echo: "You are my home."
We've traveled wide and long
and the heart is still aimed at home.
Neighbor, don't stray.
My path leads to Baghdad.

31/3/1973

ON L'AKHDAR AGAIN

Once they asked two stars:
Why don't you, some night,
become a single star?
Once they asked a star:
Why don't you, someday,
become two stars?

When heavy iron presses
on the hanging place in my neck
on the protruding knot
behind my throat, tell me then,
you loquacious L'Akhdar,
where will that city be?
The city that belonged to the Qarawites,
those alleys and the crossing to Córdoba?
Tell Tahar Ben Jelloun
and Laabi,
tell Ali Yetta and the plague-ridden newspapers
— *Le Petit Morocain* —
should I swim by the fishing harbor
or should I swim on the beach,
where the Alawites build their homes
and their secret lives?

You come to see me.
Your face is my law.
Do you love Malika?
Fatima?
The hippie women who flock to Marrakech?
Are you smuggling arms in the Rif now?
Was your pistol French?
Spanish?
Russian?
Or was it an orphaned stone from the desert?

Say: The Berber built our civilization.
Say: The revolution among nationality X
will rise from interaction with nationality Y.
Say: The scoundrels
and the women and the soldiers come to Casablanca
with news of ships filled with tourists
and yellow tobacco
and bottles no one drinks.
Say: The elevator was damaged.
Say: The girl at the bar is watching us.
Say: The man talking to you is imagining
a flower on trial.

But. . . .
What will you say about the murdered,
the ones who were hung
and the woman in a wedding gown dancing
with a rope . . .
and about the mountain you were bestowed
and your land?
Will having a nuclear weapon calm you?
So that you turn that mountain into
a desert for nomads to roam after the war turns it
into trampled earth.

Say:
The star was one.
The star has gone back to being one
and all people are equal
and the revolution is successful
and the workers have their recreational facility.
And they are led by a man who knows how
to knead words and how to put down strikes. . . .
Tens of cars to the union leaders

and tens of bribes.
Have we miscounted?

Shall we return then
to pure poetry tonight,
to docile literature?

Once they asked two stars:
Why don't you, some night,
become a single star?
Once they asked a star:
Why don't you, someday,
become two stars?

21/6/1974

THE COLLAPSE OF THE TWO-RIVERS HOTEL

The desert is not far from it,
and when the date palms sway into its rooms,
it becomes dusty like the water
of the nearby river and the old pipes.
Its three floors were built of gypsum and lime.
The windows with thick English glass open
to the garden bar and boats.
Maybe the drive here is shorter
if you take the right turn instead. . . .
Maybe you would think: How beautiful
these gardens are.
In the Two-Rivers Hotel
we loved and gambled
and learned how to maneuver
around the poisonous liquors served in its rooms.
One day we married
and came back after the years reeled us.
We came dragging our children
to show them its gardens . . .
and we were worn by what we carried.
We didn't know about the gypsum and the lime. . . .
We didn't feel the water dripping . . .
and the roof. . . .
Ah, after the years reeled us
we came back dragging our children
to show them its gardens . . .
and we were worn by what we carried.

25/6/1974

NOONTIME

Between desiring
and walking together
there is a field for hesitation
                              or reflection
                                        or boredom.

Think about it:
Can we talk in a restaurant
or find a river to dip our hands in?
Or should we be content with breathing,
or let ourselves be snuffed out by a question?

Still, when I see you I remain
anxious,
shy,
holding the tip of a thread,
waiting in the shade.

   1975

HOUSE OF MIRTH

Ah, my friend whom I loved
has turned to dust.
Will I lie like him
and not rise ever again?

Mistress of the tavern,
as I look at your face,
will I never see the death
I dread and fear?

GILGAMESH

Camphor trees blossom
with birds
and camphor trees blossom
with dubious smells as the street blurs
in humid evenings and trees.

The walls are branches
and the asphalt a country road
where the river shines
on license plates
and on the dress of a girl passing by. . . .

The house was on the corner.
Behind its windows it hid
the sleeplessness of past nights
or the sleeplessness of coming nights
or the dress of a girl torn off
in the sleeplessness of past nights
or the sleeplessness of coming nights
or in the backseat of a car.
. . . .
. . . .

Camphor trees:
a green lantern by the door of the house
and women's panties among the branches.
The oleander trees
are shielded by the steady night
and banknotes
and deals.
And the trees hold all the street's autumn,
clinging to their yellowed leaves
with the bark of their ripped trunks.
They swing their graves in secret
and open treacherous eyes to the owls.
They scrutinize the door of the house:
the girls come
and go.
The cars come
and
go.
Night comes
and the girls' eyes, night dust
and water heavy with salt
carried off on speeding wheels.
. . . .
. . . .

Inside, the masters of night enter
with the solitude of night chill
and the last betrayers of night
and bouquets of oleander flowers.

13/1/1975

SOLITUDE

One morning I saw them hurrying by,
walking together,
the scent of almonds filling the street.
Are they sisters?
I noticed their practiced cat steps.
Why did I feel the scent of almonds following me
and that I knew something about two sisters
walking the morning in a hurry?
Every morning
when the clock strikes ten, I worry.
Will they pass by?
They pass by
and I catch the scent of almonds
and I touch the soft side of a cat's paw.
Then they disappear among the trees
or around the bend
or in the last angle of my window.
Sometimes they turn back
and I see a thread
connecting my room
to everything.

15/1/1975

THE NEW BAGHDAD

She comes to me with a bowl of soup
when I am besieged by
fumes
                        of cheap arak.
She comes to me in dusty noons.
And with each sunset night snatches
she comes to me with
                        an evening star.

In the cafés she sits to bitter tea.
In the market she sells cheese
and buffalo livers.
She dusts her used-clothing stores,
searching for bones in a bowl of soup,
for milk to the lips of a child
and a glimmer in a pair of eyes
and something a woman does not yet know
and streets where water never greens.

At night
she roams among houses abandoned by the poor
and churches where a muffled mass fades
and huts where poor girls faint.
At midnight
she returns to her enchanted shelter
behind muddy streets,
carrying the bread of the dead,
myrtle flowers,
slivers of buffalo liver
and two bones for a bowl of soup.

At dawn she stops by all her houses,
waking all her children,
dragging them to the street,
the thousands waiting to march on Baghdad.

8/4/1975

THE FORESTS

Twice I ended up in a forest.
Once, I yielded to childhood friends,
eyes that held secrets and the mystery of time,
palm fronds, and hands I held,
muddy clothes, and a few songs.

Then I ended up in a forest.
The eyes I used to read were shut away
from the sky of childhood.
The hands I held carried
sticks made for pain,
and the branches were rifles.

Where are our muddied clothes?
Did the songs leave us?
Have we been beaten by marching tunes?

Forest of childhood,
how did we surrender to you,
and how did we end up alone,
searching for quarrels between our fingers
and places to plant our trees?
. . . .
. . . .

Twice I ended up in a forest.
Once, I yielded to childhood and to friends
and another time to myself.

16/12/1975

THE GARDENER

Since he was a child he learned
the secret of rain and its signs:
how clouds fall in the palm
and the earth despairs
(and the ants' way of lining the garden),
how roots shake in their secrets,
and the trees.

Since he was a child he learned
that when rain falls in mist
there will be no lightning at the end
of the horizon,
no thunder in the heart,
no wave on the river.

But you know that life has widened
like a cape in the wind
that will rouse the rain at night
like a herd of buffalo. . . .
The rain will fall,
no lightning at the end of the horizon,
no thunder in the heart,
no wave on the river.

*He never speaks with Palestine
except when he's sleeping.
Sometimes he walks toward it
without following a star.
The friends he loves open gates
    for him . . .
small bridges to viaducts.
He does not like oranges
but he loves orange trees.*

*In Sidi-bel-Abbès there is
    a cemetery.
On feast days it is dressed in
    white and green:
women's gowns and pine trees.
He often thought he will be
    buried in it.*

*What poem is he writing?
The air is sealed in a bottle,
the tongue a piece of wood
parched from alcohol.*

. . . .

This is how we learn
or how we speak
or how we come to belong to the trees.

17/4/1976

HOW L'AKHDAR BEN YOUSSEF WROTE HIS LAST POEM

Seven days passed and he didn't write. He read until his eyes hurt, and at noon he walked the park. At night he walked up and down the sandy beaches of Oran. His friend said: "You didn't sleep for six days. . . ." He told her: "Of all my friends, you're the only one who's remained." He, at any rate, is an unbalanced character, even if he appears calm. And because he's unbalanced, and because his mind is scattered, and because he didn't sleep for six days . . . he couldn't write a poem. Still, he took down these notes, fearing he'll forget them.

Notes
— Do not turn your jacket over even if it's worn out.
— Search for your defeated ring in your victorious country.
— Do not live in the words of exile when the house becomes too small.
— Do not eat the flesh of your enemy.
— Do not drink the sweat on your brow.
— Do not bite the hand that feeds you flowers.
— A guest may have the house, but not the people of the house.
— He who asks shall receive anything, but love.
— In old age gray hair may look black.
— All betrayals begin with a woman.

Fine. Here is L'Akhdar Ben Youssef facing a task more complicated than he imagined. It's true that when he wrote a poem he thought very little of what will happen to it. Still, writing becomes easy when one can concentrate on a thing, a moment, a shiver, a leaf of grass. . . . Now, however, he's confronted with ten commandments and he doesn't know which to pick. . . . And more important than all of this, how to begin? Endings are always open, beginnings are always closed.

Do Not Live in the Words of Exile
When the House Becomes Too Small

Waves gush between his hands.
He grabs a stone (suddenly) and turns it into a shell.
He remains listening;
a wind gust (constant) blows, blows constantly.
He enters the elements.
All the sea holds becomes a giant wave.
All the earth holds becomes a giant wave.
And he enters the elements:
a clenched fist,
a stone,
and a face with embossed features.
Here he is in his familiar streets . . .
his steps quickened,
an oyster shell in his hand.

Is your breathing calmer now? Maybe you can still write. Since you
were twenty you often felt in danger when you started a poem. But
once you finished the first stanza you felt a power inside you, its
origins unknown to you . . . like a spring from hidden sources. You
only feel the muffled gush. It must be your belief then, I mean you,
L'Akhdar Ben Youssef, it must be your belief that you are now among
the lost.

Do Not Turn Your Jacket Over Even If It's Worn Out

A girl enters
the used-clothes
store.
She's thin.
Her eyes widen
the way a skirt widens in the wind
and widen

to stare at her lover's jacket,
his red-black jacket
and its missing buttons

He may have used a new meter here, or no meter. The issue is not important. When L'Akhdar Ben Youssef is withdrawn from the world he loses his bearings. This is why his wings remain tied to a string dragging on the face of the earth.

Search for Your Defeated Ring in Your Victorious Country
No victor at night's end, and no defeated.
Each struggles with his stumbling.
Each regrets his stupor.
Each walks to his own slaughterhouse foolish as a bee.
Search for your defeated ring in your victorious country.
That lost star . . .
maybe you'll find it.
And if you do
you'll let go of it
at the end of the night.

Finally he remembered al-Mutanabbi, an old myopic poet, standing in the sand looking for his lost ring. There are jewelers in the world, and there are artists. On the Algerian rug black is balanced with red. Between them is the color of ash. And the yellow . . . why? The yellow. Jaune! Jaune! Arthur Rimbaud or Tristan Tzara? Oh, how close yellow is to green! Only the sea. Camus used to love the yellow of the wheat fields facing the sea near Tibaza. . . . Tibaza, ah Tibaza!

In Old Age Gray Hair May Look Black
An old man at fifty
squats in his room, occupied with lies and cigarettes.

Who will return to the toothless his milk teeth?
Who will return to the grayhead the hair of his youth?
Who can fill this empty head?
But
in old age gray hair may look black
and a lie may hold the truth
and cigarette clouds can look like a sky raining
and in his toothless gums
milk teeth may grow.
But in old age too
a very old man at fifty can fall
dead in his room,
dressed in lies and smoke.

L'Akhdar Ben Youssef is still unbalanced, his mind still scattered
    because:
He hadn't slept for six days.
He couldn't write a poem.
He didn't hesitate to publish everything he wrote.

19/6/1976

NOCTURNAL

On a street with disappearing features, the last torches will be snuffed, the doors shut secretly with chains. What evening star is this that always disappears? What song are we muffling? Candles drip in the garden where a child swallows river mud. . . . Fly, dove, awhile and your branch will disappear. A candle fell. I got tired of wearing my features, a granite face was spinning, a street that had lost its features now darkens, and darkens. . . . It disappears in dust, and clouds in my eyes. I pave my memory with its broken stones.

The waters that flooded his grave were a soft salt. The boy watched the comets' glittering explosions. Women cried, and the orphaned child flew in his first car ride. Why do the girls mention his father's name? Youssef, Youssef? A woman recognized him and he kissed her cheek. The floodwaters were a soft salt and the date palms were white and the boy watched the comets' glittering explosions. The girls' bewitcher, your uncle, he used to shoot comets from his hands. At noon the girls scream Youssef's name. His mud tomb sinks in floodwaters, and screams, and glittering comets.

If I had a tower, I would live in it alone.
If I had a palace, I would bring dogs to guard me alone.
If I had two women, I would choose one and live for her alone.
If my steps were to tread on water,
I would walk to the ends of the earth alone.

5/10/1976

ENEMIES

A poem in three movements

1. Childhood

Through cardamom flower beds,
through papyrus, through orchards of falling dates,
we walk,
a stream trickling between forehead and mouth. . . .
Air filled with the smell of wild boar
hangs on our clothes.
We clutch palm fronds
and our ancestors' rifles are handmade.
The wild boar swims on green clouds.
Morning crumbs are still under our fingernails,
and the eyes of our orphans search
through cardamom flowers,
through papyrus,
through bilharzia,
for driftwood tossed by passing ships
and search those ships for a meaning to the sea.
A sailor waves
and we lift our muddied clothes:
Greetings, god of driftwood,
god of floating cans.
Seagulls rummage through garbage on the shore.
The wild boar rustles in the congested chest.
A spot of water reddens. . . .
We piss blood
and laugh
and the wild boar rustles through the papyrus.
I call to shore:
Aunt, my aunt, O aunt. . . .
Where are our ancestors' handmade rifles?
The boar rustles in the mud.
We were orphans
searching for a meaning to the sea.

Things touched us but we didn't learn.
Names touched us but we didn't speak.
These blunt palm fronds are children's toys
and the smell of bread
and the roof of the reed hut by the shore.
Aunt, my aunt, O aunt....
These green fronds!
And the boar swims
through green clouds
and a red spot appears on the water
between papyrus and children's feet.
The god of the sea disappears
and the last waves from his ship
pull us to driftwood and tossed cans.
The head spins,
the head with burned hair,
the head with burned eyes.
And the sun spins....
The sea-sun falls into the head aching underwater
and the wild boar leaves his hiding place among green clouds,
following the sun sphere aching into the water....
The wild boar rustles
between driftwood and tossed cans.
By the shore our orphans' eyes glare at pieces of bread
and at the head aching underwater.
The wild boar writhes in the red water.
Aunt, my aunt, O aunt....

2. Insurgency

A plane rains quails made of paper,
a manna of words we do not comprehend.
We grab them happy and shivering,
a country we forget what to call....

We know that I-R-A-Q are letters we pronounce
but where can we see it?
Will it enter through the door of our reed hut someday?
Will it come carrying clay pots
filled with fresh buttermilk
or white butter?
A plane drops paper quails
and circles the date palms,
draping them with words we do not comprehend. . . .
Abdelhassan Ben Mubarak gathered ten pots
for the quails and the manna
and Abdelhassan Ben Mubarak told us:
Tonight we'll eat.
The consolation plane passes
on the tops of the palms
like a black pig. . . .
We are poor youths walking the land
of an I-R-A-Q we do not know.
Tonight we'll eat. . . .
Abdelhassan Ben Mubarak takes us to the shore,
ten pots to his left side.
A plane like a black pig
circles the tops of the palms
and Abdelhassan Ben Mubarak leads us naked to water.
He cries out to us:
Tonight we'll eat. Come to your senses.
The waters were rising
and the red tide was filled with fish.
A plane
like a shark
circled above the water,
and Abdelhassan Ben Mubarak, naked, led us in.
Tonight we'll eat.

We carried pots for manna
and the red tide carried fish we craved
and the fishermen on the other bank
and the shark
plane passed over the shore.
We fell into the warm water
naked
and alone
and we were carrying pots for the quails
and words we didn't comprehend
and Ben Mubarak's I-R-A-Q.
The sides of the fish were soft against our scaly skin.
Abdelhassan Ben Mubarak shouted,
K-A-W-S-A-J,
K-A-W-S-A-J,
shark…
shark….
The black fin rose like an axe over the water
and a plane like a wild boar
like a shark
passed over the water.
We, the poor youths, screamed.
We, the walkers of an I-R-A-Q we do not know, screamed. …
And we, poor youths, hurried back to the shore,
the black fin like an axe hovering over the water,
and Abdelhassan Ben Mubarak screamed,
his flesh torn,
and the red water reddened and reddened
and Abdelhassan Ben Mubarak fell
toward disfigurement
and the shark rushed toward the white water. …
A plane passing over an I-R-A-Q we do not know.

3. Days of 1963

I sleep in Sibah.
The guard across the bars was kind.
He was ill,
      withdrawn,
            a stranger.
Poor youths roamed desert houses
and houses in sorrowful towns.
They were carried in trucks that tossed them about,
chained two to two.
The pig-plane-shark watched over them.
Which I-R-A-Q will rise in Sibah?
Last night "the station" was filled.
The youths sang until the wild boar screamed.
The wild boar rustled across the bars.
The wild boar has two fangs made of steel.
The river ran along the right corner of the station.
A long time ago a man came here
searching for the Creator's tree.
A long time ago the poisoned water was a refuge.
Lovers hid in esparto grass.
Behind the palms, on the other bank, oil fumes rose.
The shark-oil-tanker had the scent of wild boar,
the glimmer of the black plane.
We sing in the holding station:
Where is the tavern girl?
A gun smuggler runs a bar under his blanket.
Iranian workers sleep tonight in the square.
At midnight the village comes carrying flaming fronds
and sacrifices of bread
and offerings of dates.
Iranian workers sleep tonight in the square.
Oil fumes on the other bank . . .

behind the palms and the temples of Zara
and the Iranian workers asleep in the square.
His visit was denied.
His wife will wrap her cape around her,
holding his clemency papers.
His wife sits in a corner, her eyes smiling.
He tries to look at her eyes.
A machine gun from the station roof watches him.
Where is the tavern girl?

I sleep in Sibah.
The wild boar was on "the station" roof.
And the poor youths roamed
through houses in sorrowful towns.
They were carried in trucks
that tossed them about,
chained two to two.

Baghdad, 1977

THE PORCUPINE

He lives in his old continent
alone,
cramped between sun dust and evening grass,
his white stomach taut as a bowstring.
He watches for the stitching of ants
and the shiver of water seeping through branches.
His eyes seek what a child touches as it goes mad
or what night wears as it goes mad
or what befalls the trees
or what the trees bear. . . .

The porcupine
hiding in this great drowsiness
is taken by the things of his old continent.
Children once mistook him
for a rag ball to play with,
a woman believed he was a rock
to massage her feet with,
and when it wandered into his hole
a palm snake thought him a stiff mouse. . . .

Night begins
in his old continent
and the porcupine moves
slowly
with laughing eyes,
glad the earth is full
of these temptations.

Baghdad, 1979

Algeria
1980

FIRST SNOW

First snow swarms the street;
its flakes speckle the trees,
and the girls' cheeks redden.
Who can ask a flower how it bloomed?
Snow tumbles
and the fallen leaves swirl.
Snow . . .
and you pass by, warm,
wrapped in your leather coat
until the street ends.

Snow . . .
and on your writing papers
the girls' cheeks redden.

Batna, 17/3/1980

THE FLAGS

One afternoon in the corner of a store
I found a bundle of flags.
Weren't they leaning on the wall
and wasn't the wall damp?
I said: "As long as I am here
and while the store owner
is paying them no mind,
why don't I take them out in the sun
and let them flutter for a while?
Maybe the mildew on the sticks will fall off
or they will dry in the sun
and someone passing by may see them
and someone stumbling by may see. . . .
Maybe I'll choose one and carry it
and see the glorious colors wave in the wind."
I reached out my hand,
but in my rush to hold one
it fell
and crumbled into
suffocating
dust
that chased me out of the lethargy of the store,
out of the dank corner
and its flags,
out of the rusted gate.

Batna, 25/3/1980

THE VILLAGE

Yesterday, he chose a corner
to read his documents
and fingered what the lines read:
his age,
the years,
the young face, and his village.
He felt the earth fixed under his feet —
the water still running
and the bridge still small.
Then suddenly . . .
a childhood song touched him.
Will L'Akhdar, stuttering now,
say anything after all?
And the steps?
Should he let his feet go
wherever they wish?
. . . .
. . . .
. . . .

In the distance his village,
its bridge,
the oleander tree,
the childhood song,
and the road to his hands.
. . . .
. . . .
. . . .

His only suitcase was a trifle:
bottles of wine,
papers, a striped suit,
and a song to the song of childhood.
. . . .
. . . .
. . . .

He didn't see the old house
or the café.
In the distance he didn't see
the oleander tree.
And at the bridge
the people had gouged eyes.

Batna, 25/3/1980

POETRY

Who broke these mirrors
and tossed them
shard
by shard
among the branches?
And now...
shall we ask L'Akhdar to come and see?
Colors are all muddled up
and the image is entangled
with the thing
and the eyes burn.
L'Akhdar must gather these mirrors
on his palm
and match the pieces together
any way he likes
and preserve
the memory of the branch.

Batna, 26/3/1980

THE VISIT

When he visited Iraq
he didn't travel much.
They said:
"This L'Akhdar is arrogant. . . ."
They told him:
"So many have spread out in this land
and many were truly lost.
But you, a mere spectator,
didn't lose a day
and you were not lost."
He replied:
"The land is for its people.
This land is not my land,
and its people are not mine.
And water is not sky."

Batna, 26/3/1980

APRIL STORK

He arrived like this . . .
without drums or marching band.
He arrived tired and quiet.
The first decision: choosing a house.
The second: the straw that will make the nest.
The third: the nest. . . .
But the city
is still in ruins. . . .
It does not know why he came,
will not know what he will do,
will not notice him
when departure calls on him.

Ratna, 3/5/1980

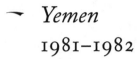 *Yemen*
1981–1982

SCENE

The nets hang to dry
and the fisherman is busy
among a thousand chores.
The boat rests on the dry sand.
The gulls form a white line on the water,
the crows a black line on the sand.
On the boat a crow lands and a gull alights,
while Slavic bodies strip
and stumble
between sea and sand.

Aden, 31/1/1981

SUMMER

An African summer at the beach,
a summer of Oran.
If my memory of greenery were to cloud up,
I would see the mountains of Aden
like a giant harbor glittering.
The children swim
and the Slavic women swim.
And you, in your woolen burnoose,
are you keeping warm in a winter
you made for yourself?

Aden, 31/1/1981

SPARROWS

This morning I saw a sparrow
on a thin stalk of yellow corn,
the only plant adorning
the seaside hotel.
The sparrow cleaned itself;
the stalk shook.
Another sparrow came;
the stalk bent.
A third sparrow;
the stalk bowed quickly.
Then suddenly,
and in unison,
the three sparrows took off,
leaving the hotel.
And under my shirt
a thousand sparrows
shivered.

The Gold Coast, Yemen 1/2/1981

A MOMENT

I love you caught
waiting,
flustered
like a leaf before rain.
I love you stuttering
even as you say:
"Good morning."
How can one know
on which morning
the shot will be fired?
Or which drop
will fall alone,
delicate
with
the surprise of expectation?

15/4/1981

THE SPRING

1.

Back to the wall, and the bullet waits. Nothing on your back except
the tattoos of the Arab cement, the floor of the cell and the shoes of
the young man who specializes in breaking vertebrae. The bullet
waits. . . . You who have fortified eyes . . . the sky is low . . . the sky is
narrow. Like a stone on a rose. And you in the distance between
stones and roses, open your eyes. . . . The guard takes you to the
shooting range. You shoot at the stone profile. . . . And the remaining
shots fly like birds toward sea and star. Time in a bottleneck. And the
mastery is only in negotiating with murder. The squabbling ranks
have not settled their scores. This is why you escaped death's tested
formula. Back to the wall, and the bullet waits. Keep your eyes open
in the blink of astonishment. Leave a space for dreaming, even as
small as a bullet.

I return to the sea once again
as if I held Aden in my summer shirt pocket.
Will the birds find a cave in the sea?
Will the girl find a bed among the stones?
Will the fighter find a trench?
But to the sea, to this sea, I return
with Aden in my summer shirt pocket
and I touch it as if touching a woman from the coast
and white domes
and my kin who have gone away. . . .
My blood cries to me:
I am returning to the sea,
holding Aden in my summer shirt pocket,
carrying it like a magician's rose.
And I tell lovers: "This is my rose.
Come to the sea.
Its skies are mother-of-pearl.
Its scents are red. . . ."

2.

I name your Arab face after the soil. I name you "Sword Belt" from
unknown shores. I name you scattered husk between straits
and stones. I name you and your absence. I pronounce you in the
languidness of slippery moments.
Who will give us our mothers' names? Who will leave
an albatross feather on the pillow? This is how we rise
in the morning of legends: we wash our hands of beliefs. . . .
And we say: "Here, we are saints, innocent as sand." We say:
"Galilee belongs to us and we are not ashamed."
In the morning of legends, words are bodies.
I will not deride the revolution. Ships dig
into the Mandab Strait, and the bird is higher than the mountain. Once,
as we sat among fishermen in Beirut, a Palestinian girl told me:
"From here come the enemies' planes." Her index finger
pointed at the whole world.

Amman in San'a, or Ajman in Beirut,
or Baghdad a ringed orchard,
names of cities emptied and their impressions entangled.
Their alphabets have forgotten their shapes and their shapers.
They will make us forget those lands and their weeds
and God and the earths and our births.
They will make us forget veins that tied rib to rib
and the Arab in the hidden star
and the boy playing with toys made for his offspring.
But I hide for the young girl another rose.
I say: "Dhafar. . . ."
My song flies with the wings of the women of Oman
with clothes of kohl and narcissus
and a meaning for "against"
and a meaning for "foe,"
a meaning for spears and tender twigs.

Or I will listen to an oud being thrummed
in Aden
from Aden
to Aden
from Najd to Yemen.
I keep for the boys another rose.
I draw it on alley gates and sailor suits.
I chisel it on stone when I imagine trees.
I scratch it on trees when I remember stone.
I open it:
I count a petal for *ʿAyn*,
a petal for *Dāl,*
a petal for *Nun.*
Then I am in Aden
and in Aden I keep for the girls of Oman another rose.

3.

We grapple for rain as if it were the legs of a gazelle. Al-Hallaj
        is head of state.
And between us the earth's treasures and a stationary cloud.
Country that has shrunk, country that has passed away, we offered
        you
an identity card and sat you at our table. We hung you
as a poster in Fakhani and sat to guard you with the rifles of the
        poor.
We planted you like a flower in a hand grenade. And we said we will
        not
plant lightning. It is your choice. Come live in our crumpling rooms.
Come walk the last street with us. The table is set for us in Damur.
Drink the last drink with us. Drink this drink
or we will sip it until you die, then break it on your head.

Like this water, you're negligible.
You come in the supplication of imploring hands
or on coal black lips
or like ivy stretching between the bower of vision and Samarra.
Like water, you're negligible,
living between Lahaj and Mukalla
in the drains that lost their wells
and turn in the labyrinth of loss.
Like water, you're negligible.
You shiver to reach a star.
You find a nebula in a drop of water
as if between water and the universe lay the secret of the first sleep,
the first shiver.
Fingers reach out . . .
suddenly
and the lips tremble:
under the boys' feet lies the groan
of the spring.

    4.

In a seashell you listen for nymphs calling.
In a grain of sand you plant purple flowers. What a country!
It takes you, and it is not taken. Like a star it only fits in your eyes.
Like a song coming nearer. A dancer with a small shield.
A curled-up dagger turns the square into a ship
and the women are mere eyes. Embroidered like Christmas trees,
where are your houses, women of Hadramout?

From now on I will belong to Dammoun. . . .
And I say: "Tomorrow is another matter." In my wicker suitcase a
    whiff
of a secret arak distilled in the valley.
Let's hide behind the copper and sandalwood gate.

Let's hide in the saint's foyer.
Let's hide a minute. . . .
I want to love you.
I want to scratch your arm to know my blood. . . .

And I want to rest in the goodness of Yemen.
I want to find the tree where the first ancestor loosened his knotted
    tresses.
I want to light the first feather.
Maybe that lightning will bring down a cloud from the land of
    the djinn.
Will I live in the goodness of Yemen?
A month, so that it will infuse me
and weave from the threads of my summer shirt a shawl
and expose my chest to a purple star.
Is it time that I have in the goodness of Yemen
a branch,
a cot to lie in,
a native script,
and a stone to shimmer in my eye?

Aden, 20/3/1982

Beirut
1979–1982

IMMERSION

Who is the woman in Beirut killing
L'Akhdar Ben Youssef tonight?
Who is conspiring against him in a bar?
Who is killing him on the street corner,
in the corner of the café,
in the shadows,
or at the turn where no help can reach him?
Who hands him
away to be stabbed
then to be anointed with orange blossoms?

We're finished with all he had to say.
What he believed to be a star, we now understand.
And whatever house he had, we have seen it.
And that first beach, the magical sands of youth,
is now abandoned . . .
bones of birds and fish and stones that crumble. . . .
But the banter that still quivers in L'Akhdar is tempting
and that star,
that house,
that abandoned beach
are magical in L'Akhdar's eyes . . .
that banter,
that cursed burning drop
in the bottom of his last drink.

L'Akhdar sits at the bar
as he has always done
alone.

Why did I come to see him tonight?
Did I think of the drinks he swigged until . . .
— But I waited

to see him wake one day?
Did I wake him up?
— No.

In a while the street will empty
and in the orchard the light will dim.
In his room he hears the sound of footsteps.
Another night comes
and a woman walks by, carrying flowers
and wearing funeral clothes.

When the murderers came
my master L'Akhdar was not in his shelter. . . .
He was a blazing lotus tree
vowing to return,
and the world was anointed with orange blossoms.

Beirut, 7/4/1979

A FRIENDSHIP

For Adonis

When I extend my hand to you
you only shake my fingers.

When your hand reaches out
how can I hold only your fingers?

We who were raised in innocence
and sowed innocence,
we who long for no past innocence
or future innocence,
we are the children of that liquid
trapped between two seas,
children of those who hammer
at the wall until dawn
and find gypsies resting
against the other side.

A quarter of a century since then
and we arrive to find
that Ibn Taymiya has turned
into the head of a bludgeon
and al-Muwafaq is still cleaving
rebellious slaves
from the womb of the earth.
The police of Damascus kick us
and the police of Iraq
and the Arabs' American police
and the English
and the French
and the Persian
and the Ottoman police
and the police of the Fátimide caliphs. . . .
Our families

kick us,
our naive, good-hearted families,
our murderous families.

We are the children of this madness.
Let's be whatever we wish.

What we share is not trust.
We share the throat of the bleeding flower.
Between us the storm emerges
from its elements. . . .
I say: "Let's shake hands."

Beirut, 8/4/1979

DAYS OF JUNE

In a sour morning a soldier grabs his rifle
and smashes it on a tree.
In a sour morning Khalil Hawi grabs his rifle
and smashes it on his head.
In a sour morning S. drinks his tea alone.
This is how these sour mornings pass,
living tissues leavening,
the sun a muddle,
the sea fogged up,
and the record spins around itself
like the newspapers,
like the PLO,
like Sinnin water,
and civilian planes
and anti-Marxist think tanks
and the ideal methods for two bodies to join.
The tree near my window doesn't want to spin.
The sea has no wish to soften into green.
The passersby have no desire to walk on.
And I stutter here in secret like a swing
seeking the water in the trees,
hoping the sea will soften to green,
the sea that will rise to my window.
I will move lightly to spinning terraces.
But what makes the noon light glow this way,
heavy with vapors and empty bottles?
Who invited one of the enemy's colonels
to sit on the low chair?
Who taught the pig how to eat flowers?
And this roaring from Palestinian skies —
is it bearing the rockets of judgment day?
Noon is hot and bloated
like a ram tied to

a ragged tree.
Noon shuts the inflamed eyes of a dog.
Noon stretches on the sea
like a whale that has been dead for days.
And in the refugees' thousand-story hotels
the smells of winter socks,
milk,
vegetable oil,
and distant fields.
Noon throbs
and when the jet fighters pass overhead,
roaring,
a small vein throbs
between my temples and eyes,
and this small space between the cigarette
and the ashtray throbs.
When the planes fly over
pieces of shrapnel lodge in the soul.
Then it becomes
the spirit of a counterfeit god,
an Israelite god,
an ugly god.
I do not want to see you on another evening.
I want to see you this evening, this evening only.
The boat like a warship,
the warship like a warship.
There is the tree and there is the warship.
Maryam's coat and a warship.
The evening alone with a warship.
Isn't she the one who slipped away from Cherbourg one evening
to cross the Gibraltar Strait while an Arab king watched her?
This evening is red. Is it Dante's cloud?
I want to see you this evening. . . .

To the thirty shells per minute,
to the houses that crumble,
to the eyes that look out or grow dim,
to the strewn tombs,
to the saplings choking in ash,
to the refugee camp isolated like an island nation,
we draw a circle,
we draw a fumbling nation,
then drag it
into the air of the trenches.

Beirut, 15/7/1982

MARYAM COMES

1.

In a moment she covered you with kisses
and when she left she was crowned with a white straw hat.
In which river will her fingers dip?
Which water will drench her shirt?
By which date palm will she rest her back?
Will the ripe dates fall?
Will shaking the palm trunk be all that Maryam does?
The trees are music
and this whitewashed apartment in Beirut still faces the sea.
In the distance another coastal city looms.
I see my grandfather's face: the blue eyes, the red kaffiyeh.
Through barricades I see Maryam's face.
And across the axis-lines echo the footsteps
of a king crowned with a rocket.
The Romans enter orderly in a regiment
while nationalists murder each other in the stores.
Maryam in her city
and you watch the distant roads: will she come today?
She was at the street garbage dump
and she lit her fires.
Then, crowned in fumes, she left
and the city was blessed.

My heart is with you, ablaze
at night behind the sand fortifications.
Can hope palpitate without you?
Was the horse stable throbbing?
Every house you come to, you remember another house.
Whenever you felt alive, you forgot the dead.
But what you've come to now is not what you were.
Nothing is left for me.
Nothing left for me except a shade.

So be it.
A passing shadow
is the best that can be hoped for in the parade of exodus.

2.

If I know where Maryam is
I will follow a star to reach her land.
But Maryam left me in a labyrinth when she departed.
She said: "You will find me if you love me."
In sand I search for her fingers.
In the black ruins of Ain el-Hilwa I look for her eyes.
At the door of "the agency" I ask the young men: "Did she come?"
And between the pages of newspapers I search for clues.
On the radio, yesterday, I heard a voice:
Maryam's voice.
Is she living among the "explosions" between Lailki and Sullam?
Beirut, against whose stones I rest my back,
Beirut is startled like a seabird
and the lovers swing their machine guns
and the sea calms.
The children listen for a treacherous sound
and in the distance fires break
and planes gyrate in a leaden horizon.
For you, Maryam, lovers and explosions.
Are you coming then?
Come. . . .
This space, we will continue to knock on its door
until we reach the flag that rises in depravity,
until the released bird heads for the stars
to release our caged vows.
Palestine in the prairie, trapped in shelters
in the thick floods of bullets,
in the voice of the stone thrower.

Palestine in songs, in the coal black tress,
in the martyr's shirt,
in iron hurled at iron,
in a hand,
in an arm,
in the country coming toward us.

3.

Here we are, Maryam, plotting our escape in overcast night,
watching for the bullets that follow us,
and like two terrorized birds we jump
between a rocket and another.
Here we are, Maryam, descending the staircase to the shelter.
We count the raiding planes
and we say: "We believe,"
and we walk in secrecy to the sea.
We sit behind the sandbags
and watch the waves crash and the young fighters.
Their clothes are greened like the rocks on Mediterranean shores.
Wait a little, let's say "Peace" to them.
Let us bless their weapons with tears.
Let us wash our hair with scarce water
and chew on hard bread in silence.

Maryam, mirror and vision,
a prophecy that we will die in honor
and that we will live the way simple friends live.
Maryam lives in nativity,
she lives in Arab blood.
We follow her and she follows us,
but here in these cruel moments
we weave our identity from her clothes
and proceed to the day of judgment.

From a stone foundation our flag rises,
planted in the stoppage of time.
We will plant it and replant it
until we burst this nation's spring.

Let what is to be come.
Let madness come.
Let it.
We are bound to arrive.

Beirut, 25/7/1982

from DAILY CHORES

*(From a sequence written during the
Israeli siege of Beirut, 1982)*

A Raid

The room shivers
from distant explosions.
The curtains shiver.
Then the heart shivers.
Why are you in the midst of all this shivering?

Water

A lark drinks,
a star drinks,
the sea drinks,
and the bird
and the houseplant drinks
and the children of Sabra drink
the smoke of exploded shells.

A Room

Nothing in it except
a bookcase,
a bed,
a poster.
A jet fighter flies overhead,
lifts the bed in the air
and the last book
and tears with a rocket
part of the poster.

Electricity

Suddenly we remember night in the villages
and orchards
and going to bed at eight.
Suddenly we learn the use of dawn.

We hear the muezzin's call
and the rooster's
and the peaceful village.

Where
Where does this boy go
on this strange evening?
A water bottle and a grenade
tacked to his wide belt
and the weapon that never leaves him?
Does he head for the sea?

Ah, this strange boy!

Radio
In dump grounds or in palaces
the radio comes with us
between teacups passed around,
and explosions here and there.
We may sing a little.
We may hope a little.
And our radio remains
like the bugle of judgment day.

Rations
What are we going to buy with them?
Isn't it enough to have one shirt,
an old pair of jeans,
half a loaf of bread and cheese,
and flowers we pick from behind the fence?
What are we going to buy with them?
Maybe a moment of solidarity.

Artillery
It thunders at dawn
and the sea encircles the city like smoke.
It thunders at dawn
and a bird is frightened.
Are the planes here?

In the empty apartment
the plant falls silently
and the dishes shiver.

Beirut, June–August / 1982

Damascus / Aden / Tunis /
Nicosia / Belgrade
1983–1989

INHERITANCE

One drop,
one drop then another.
Drops stream down this window
like exclamation points. . . .
A short while, and April will depart
like an
explorer
loaded with spirits and fragrances,
leaving the exclamation points to dust,
leaving me to existence.

Damascus, 18/4/1983

THE ORCHARD

We spread ourselves by the river
and sit
listening to the fairies playing with the fish
and we hear, like bugles, the crawling of the ants
and we sense a root stretching its fingers bulging with water
and how the sun twists the veins of a leaf.

We spread ourselves by the river
and we lie down.
The fairies come to look at us
and the ants come
and the root comes
and the sun comes
and the sleeping body fills with their touch.

We spread ourselves in the café
and sit
but
will we ever reach that orchard?

Damascus, 20/4/1983

ABOUT THAT LIZARD, ABOUT THIS NIGHT

Tonight the sea is beyond the window's reach,
not even the sound of the sea,
not even a crate waiting to be emptied in the sea.
Is it the wind I'm hearing
or a scream in the lemon blossoms yellowing?
I saw towering trees,
waiting for a woman who painted her thighs green. . . .
Who will come tonight?
Who will respond to this invitation?
No. . . . No, she won't come,
won't come. . . .
The sea peeping through my window now won't be here.
And the river embedded in my fingernails
will not be here,
(its blood is clotting
the way harbor air
clots in a seashell).
So why should you come?
Why should I wait for anyone to come?

Tonight
I send five postcards to the crayfish in the sand.
I send mimosa flowers to a snake.
I send pimps to paradise.
I send condoms to the saints.
I send my sons to murdered mermaids.
(Dear God, grant me
whatever you wish.
Grant me a storm.)
She's not coming tonight.
I'll say I love you
and you still won't come.
O my Foe!   O my Foe!

O m-y F-o-e!　　O m-y F-o-e !
Tonight
I'll borrow her apartment for a while,
then leave.
Under my cotton pillow I will place
a Magnum pistol
and seven bullets.
I will leave trace bombs
and drops of night sweat.
I will leave an orchard at her door,
then I will walk to Katmandu.
In Katmandu I'll sit in Buddhist circles
and catch the first rays of daylight under a fig tree
and smoke seven cigarettes
and say: "Maybe you'll come. . . ."
(I won't say: "I'm going with her.")

I will walk to Timbuktu.
I will sit possessed under the mud arcades.
I will drink angel-water from a calabash
and I will say: "Maybe you'll come."
(Will I stay here till I die,
watching the boats sail?)

I will walk to Baghdad.
I'll sit by the river for a little while
and tour Bab al-Shaikh awhile,
then leave with a few belongings.
. . . .
. . . .
The end of the storm.
The beginning of the storm.

I will walk to Jerusalem
and I'll take down your names,
my names.
I will engrave them into the stones of the wall
and I will extend a palm of grains to a frightened pigeon.
And I will walk past myself
and I will say: "She may still come."
Hallelujah!
Hallelujah!

Aden, 30/8/1984

A FEVER

For days this wind hasn't stopped
coming at me from the sea.
All night it hallucinates.
It gives me crabs and jellyfish
in baskets made from the ropes
of sunken ships,
and shirts with a laughing tiger
imprinted on them.
All night it hallucinates
and moans.
A cat scratches at the door
and from under my bed I hear
footsteps coming . . .
. . . .
. . . .

Why do these crabs wear canvas shoes?
Who told them I am here thundered with fever?
And this cat, will he jump through the window
like a kangaroo?

Aden, 6/9/1984

A HOT NIGHT

In the air that staggers
between seashells,
the remains of a dead bird
and fish that belong to sailors
who will not return.
In the air there are these smells:
an Indian woman combed
her hair under the washline,
and the charred smell
of grilled crabs,
and this soaked shirt.

Aden, 7/9/1984

A WOMAN

How will I drag my feet to her now?
Where will I see her?
And on which street of what city
should I ask about her?
And if I find her house
(let's suppose I do)
will I ring the bell?
How should I answer back?
And how will I stare at her face
as I touch the light wine seeping
between her fingers.
How should I say hello . . .
and how will I take the pain
of all these years?

Once
twenty years ago
in an air-conditioned train
I kissed her
all night long . . .

8/9/1984

LINES

I have nothing from the heights of Rabat
except a wilting flower and a woman's dress.

Let's stay with this strange evening
and let's say you're its only light.

Which of us reached for closeness?
Which of us is deliberating with desire?

Which of us holds in his palms
anything but his dead embers?

27/10/1984

THE CHALETS BAR

Somalis and
khat sellers come to it
during the day,
and at night
the girls come
with the languages of the coast
and dresses glowing
with the colors of coastal birds.
Sometimes Frenchmen come,
and West Germans too.
And sometimes,
in your twentieth drink
twenty drunken angels fall.

Aden, 10/11/1984

SCENE

The suburban trees
are guarded with transparent fog.
They weave in secret
the clothes June will wear.
Quiet like the neighborhood seamstress,
they are startled like us when we forget,
vanishing in a similar space.

Now they are making a dress for us,
a dress whose owner has died.

Tunis, 22/1/1985

A CLOUD

You slide into my bed
the way a woman enters
a house after midnight.
But your wedding was more perfect,
two shining eyes
and a few gliding steps,
the boy's shirt, and the turn
toward the witch's place.
Then you come through languor.
You leave your thick hair to its shock
and the standing in the corner
at the tip of the circle.
Then you come through reflection.
You come in a touch,
in a premonition
to gasp before we leap
into a raining cloud.

Berlin, 30/3/1985

CRAWLING PLANT

After a year or two, I'll reach
the top of the fence.
It's the earth; it pushes me
from my roots to the top of the fence.
It's the sun; it chooses a table
and sets me there and offers its cup
overflowing with fury.
And the air that goes through me
begins to fill me as I take the last steps
to the top of the fence....
Maybe in a year or two....
But a bird that built its nest
under my arm now asks:
"Will you take these last steps
to be torn, poked, and bled
by the glass shards
at the top of the fence?"
How can I stop myself?
It's the earth and the sun
and the wind that lift me —
like this —
to the top of the fence.

Tunis, 11/5/1985

THANK YOU IMRU UL-QAIS

At last in a half-furnished room near Nicosia
you came to deliver peace on your lips.
Is it only now, after five thousand miles,
that you've found the words?
After moss filled your home
and the arrows were scattered in the sea.
Peace to a grove of figs.
Peace to this darkness.
Peace to a shell that hid its blood in wet sleep.
Peace to this ruin.

Like a spring between slim hands
slowly slipping off my covers
the way a farmer peels an apricot's soft stubble,
are you shining like silver while the world is lead?
All that surrounds me are shores.
Shall we start now?
Cities they speak of: there.
Hamlets, villages, capitals.
Our roads have diverged and crossed.
Shall we enter all exits here at once?

Shall we exit all entrances?
Our city is far
and far that eternity wounded in our eyelids.
I want your hands slim.
I won't live long, woman.

Drink me.
I won't live long, kill me.

Clouds fixed like mountains of chalk.
A swallow passes overhead
and reaches the church tower
at the end of the neighborhood.
There are three cedars there —
and I will draw them one day —
and my ashtray is full of snails.
The late morning is white
and the plant shakes
and the table shakes.
Is this the distant roar again?
Is this that blood rushing from joint to vein?
Peace to this morning bee visiting me.

When we came to measure the roads
we thought night was shorter
than Ibn Khaldun's *Muqadima*
and we said: "North Africa is our cape;
it will protect us from scorching heat and jagged cold."
Maybe we were young.
Maybe we came to eat the sour grapes
our parents avoided.
What wisdom lies in this top spinning?
Which death is easier?
(Note that we didn't even whisper:
"Which death is more beautiful?")
The cedar of the Mersa and Samarra
with the stupor of she who coiled
in a corner by her spring.

Young friends are fighting unto death
over their share of the ammunition box.
This way we go on as we were.

We learned, but what of this top spinning?
Thank you Imru ul-Qais, victim of murder.

The early sparrow sends a feather
to pomegranate blossoms.
A swallow flies, aiming
for his centimeter of the street,
and the small balconies stand
in an infinity of solitude.
Morning ended when morning arrived.
So who will come,
and who will come?
And who will color the edge of the sheet?
Who will celebrate the touch of her fingers?
Who will celebrate the astonishment of morning?
Four boats in the whiteness of the wall.
Four boats in the bottom of the ocean.

The mirrors intervene.
I wanted a voice unlike any other.
Still I proceed in the hall of mirrors:
do I close my eyes now?
Do I ignore what my eyes ignore?
This road has gone on for too long
and the mirror still interferes.
Sometimes I disappear, stumbling
in the water of small bays.
The Bosporus Strait shines before me,
in my hands grass
from the shifting bottom, and a shell.
The fish circle around, catching
butterflies, porcupines, stars,
and eyes of drowned men.

Eternal silence killing me:
where is this sound coming from?
In a while I will resume my stumbling
among mirrored halls.

Nicosia, 9/5/1986

AUTUMN

Soon the leaves will tire
of their greenness.
Drowsiness will come,
carrying its coffee
and the coffee will spill,
the papers drenched.
Morning of coffee grounds . . .
autumn branch,
morning of coffee
to grapevines and myrtle.

A cat from another world,
languid and content,
rests in her harbor-chair.
Will her pupils widen
to take in a sun dimmed
by stationary clouds?
No grasshopper on the cypress
to prick her ears for.
No sparrows.
In her chair the cat hunts down a dream
and sleeps.

The street song is hushed
and soon,
coming from fields
stripped of grass,
a crow will join us.

Nicosia, 17/10/1986

TOWER

Our cities shared their poisons with us,
then suddenly
banished us to a cloud.
We didn't despair when once again
we became fugitives. . . .
But we're no longer light as lightning
to live in a cloud again,
in any passing cloud.

In the morning we haul our crates to ports
or to baggage belts
in airport basements.

Where did you come from?

        ⌣

Where are you going?

        ⌣

How did you carry your heavy crates?

        ⌣

Did you know that the station was moved
and that the last train left twenty years ago?

        ⌣

. . . .
. . . .
. . . .

Still, I will drag my boxes
and in the evening carry them to a room.
I will climb my tower and enter
                              any room,
                                        any passing cloud.

Belgrade, 2/10/1988

CHEMICAL WEAPON

The Kurds of March were in the hush of impossibility.
Their clothes were the colors of spring,
their faces were spring,
and the singer was murdered.

The clouds that dropped black mustard in the lungs,
the clouds that looped death's throttle around a beautiful morning,
the clouds that clotted our children's blood,
the clouds that leavened Satan's bread
with the hues of twilight,
will they cross the cypress woods
and reach the date palms?

The Kurds of March were in the hush of impossibility.

Nicosia, 23/3/1989

Paris / Tunis
1989–1991

THE TREES OF ITHACA

1.

Suddenly at sunset Adam surprised us
and the world that lived within us was a palace made of glass.
Child of the moment,
Adam,
what is a moment?
And the twenty-five thorns pricking you are a crown.

~

They were not many, but they were one contingent.
Their weapons stolen like the hours of secret cells.
They crossed national borders,
nations that had no meaning.
And turbulence began.
There are princedoms of smothered wells.
There are vast kingdoms
and royal republics.
There are Palestinians without a kingdom or a republic.
The gulf waters cool the pipes of poverty
and at night village names flare.
We are farmers in Bedouin tents,
teachers who shuffle about in sandals,
merchants of confiscated goods.
We are not blind, we are not asking for bread or wine.
We turn in the earth the way a shepherd wraps his cloak around him.
But we love our dialect, and our intonations of the alphabet.
Let the continents come at us.
Let the Arab partisans come to us.
They crossed borders. These nations have no meaning. . . .
Only village names flare at night.
We will wear them like camouflage.
We will hang them on our shoulders as rifles
and shoot them with our first bullets.

And we will keep our names:
Wael Zaitar, Ghassan Kanafani, Majid Abu Sharar . . .

〜

Child of the moment,
kaffiyeh of night,
do you realize that since you came, we have not known what to do?
Is it because we are still taken by that palace of brittle glass?
Even the solitude of remembrance failed us
before the walls and their holdings collapsed. . . .
We are your cowardly brothers,
Adam.
Within your first steps we held the prison feast.
We invited you to the wolf's table
and you agreed to come, Adam,
so that you would learn. . . .
How noble you are, Adam!
You agreed to come so that you would learn.
So that we would learn.
But we, your cowardly brothers, celebrated
unavenged blood spilled on the kaffiyeh of night.
And for every knife we planted in your sweet body we picked a rose.
You transgressed, Adam.
The feast remained a prison feast.
No chorus resounded at the wolf's table
as you had hoped,
and the world that lives within us is still a palace made of glass . . .

2.

Like this, in twilight, Adam beguiled us
and the world that occupies us is a glass palace.
Child of the moment,
Adam,

what is a moment?
And the twenty-five thorns pricking you are a crown.

～

Clumps of the Sports Complex leaven like dough in the acrid air
where cluster bombs scatter like the devil's rosary.
In Chatila the roofs fly off . . .
and family photographs and the faucets of scarce water,
and from the sea to Sullam to al-Mathaf
bodies formed the battle lines.
In Alhamra we hold the festival of the poor in the thousand-star
    hotels.
This roaring coming from Khalda is our hoarded voice. . . .
The Revolutionary Council is still in place
and Abu Iyad's building is spilled on the sidewalk
and we rummage on through the universe.
No drop, no mirror.
With camouflage uniforms we go on.
With personal weapons and guns at the shore
we continue to rummage through the universe.
Weapons strapped to our flesh, give us our bread and our hands.
Give us the primal chant.
Yasir Arafat was sullen like a day riddled with explosions.
He knew the enemy had advanced
on the axis of al-Mathaf and Barbir.
The students who were fed up with their northern universities
were blazing, as if they never left their bases.
Let it roar then, the primal chant.
And let us keep our names:
Saad Sayil, Azmi al-Saghir, Ali Fouda . . .

～

Should we light the candle, Adam,
and briefly wear what we were accused of
and rise, pure like you were once. . . .
An early morning penetrates trees and wind.
An early morning, you remember, Adam:
lemons in their greenness
and lettuce leaves in elemental adornment,
a summer for songs,
for the accordion,
for waves,
for water you mixed with water. . . .
I sigh for you, Adam.
The summer was carried on a blue silver tray
and the world was a child playing in a garden
like you, Adam.
But we, your cowardly brothers, came at you with tanks,
with water from the sea,
with missiles in the wind and snipers from another kingdom. . . .
We, all of us, wanted to kill the summer that plays
and the child that tires . . .
to smash the landing of a falling wave,
fearing it will rise again.
We wanted to kill the barbarity of loin and offspring every woman
    holds within her.
We wanted to kill what the night kaffiyeh engraves on the face of
    the wind.
We wanted to kill you once, and once again, and a thousand
    times. . . .
Oh, how happy we were with our doing!
How beautiful!
But the firing squad facing you was even more beautiful.
Ah, Adam. . . .

How cruel you were when you left us behind, your cowardly
    brothers!
Stones on the beach,
stumps on shifting sands,
you, murderer dressed in the victim's clothes . . .

3.

Like this, in darkness, Adam left us
and the world that lived within us is a palace made of glass.
Child of the moment,
Adam,
what is a moment?
And the twenty-five thorns pricking you are a crown.

          ".

Here we are, wearers of kaffiyehs wrapped like helmets.
To us the chirping of bullets
and cedars falling like tears. . . .
To us the harbor song
where young boys are submerged into war chants.
To us the twenty-one-bullet salute and the new army trucks.
From the Municipal Stadium
and the Abu Shahla Square
we march like a river of songs,
"like a river of lions."
The Beretta rifle is polished in the early morning, and gleaming.
Which dew will gather on the balcony plants?
Which woman will say: "No"?
I love you like this
in the intensity of snubbing and quarrels.
We smuggled our children tucked among our bodies. . . .
The kaffiyeh is a helmet
and the face is a prophet's.

We go into the Hellenic sea to reclaim our souls.
And we will keep our names:
Laila Khaled, Mahmoud Darwish, and al-Khidr . . .

He is building boats out of the ribs of speech,
unfolding sails out of the scent of lemons,
and bringing nearer cities that were ravaged by plagues
and raiders and brothers and history. . . .

How long will it take him to cross the sea,
where there is no sea? How long will it take him to reach the earth,
where there is no earth?
How many young men will he need to conquer the known world?
A purple light spirals on the kaffiyeh of night
and gun powder . . .
and this khaki outfit,
this great journey.
Who is he saving the dust of songs for?
Who is he leading away?
Yet . . . he's leaving
and the sails, thinner than a taste of air, fill up with wind.
And the boys between shadowy stern and prow
carried grass,
flags,
and small weapons. . . .
Are you leaving so suddenly, Adam?
The sea you cut through is cutting us,
leaving us prisoners, naked without Adam.
We do not know what to do.
You were the gift, the everlasting loom.
You were night, awakening, and certainty.
Your distance held our yearning,

an assurance that the cowardly brothers will remain cowardly.
Why do you leave tonight, Adam?
Will you leave us prisoners,
having been a captive yourself?

4.

Adam did not reveal what he held secret.
                  And why speak when his eyes are conscience?
The seeds of intention, whenever he suppressed them,
              burst like grass fed by deep roots.
This is God's earth. If it were to shrink, let it.
             Let it be the last foothold.
This is God's earth and he entrusted it
             to an angel-child who walks on water.
This is God's earth, a stone of it
            will suffice. . . .

I saw al-Khidr.
I was walking and the water lifting me rose higher.
I wanted to go to the walls.
I wanted only a door. . . .
Al-Khidr said: "Come, you have reached the gate.
            Enter my garden."
I hesitated.
Al-Khidr said: "You didn't enter?"
I fell silent.
Al-Khidr said: "My son,
            he who crosses the distance,
            he who seeks water,
            he who roams this stone,
            he who pitches tents in the valley
            will enter the promised refuge."

5.

Here in Africa's high noon . . .
here under the noon stars,
let us take a rest, Adam.
Let us drink some tea and anise
and bitter coffee.
Or let us chew (as if in dream) these beans.
It does not matter.
We have reached our twenty-fifth year
and we have become skillful
and wise. . . .
The hazy trees of the Ithaca harbor appear in the distance.
Let us sit for a while . . .

Paris, 31/12/1989

CAVAFY'S HOUSE

Six Lipsius Street:
was your Alexandria the sea?
Or was it the turn
to where the alley narrows
and dispenses a flimsy light
like the gloss on boiled snails?
Maybe your Alexandria was this door
I cannot see.
Maybe it was the mumblings
that trembled at the lips
but were never released. . . .
Maybe the vase or the palace terrace
where the god forsook Anthony. . . .
Six Lipsius Street:
where did the Greeks of night come from?
Where did this wine come from?
Where is this stumbling song coming from?
And this broken bouzouki?
And this air that is Alas, Alas,
this air airing its Ah, Ah?

Six Lipsius Street:
the balcony darkens. . . .
The room withdraws
into the wardrobe mirror.
The shirt flies to the sea
and the sea is absent . . .
. . . .
. . . .

If you are Anthony,
wait then.
Maybe from the shards of the mirror
a god will rise
and call your name.

Tunis, 12/2/1990

1989

Vladimir Ilich,
what is wrong with this evening?
Which flags will rise tonight
in the square?
Which Caesars will come
donned in togas?
Which women will wake
in the morning to bells
from abandoned churches?
Vladimir Ilich,
as you prepared your treatises in exile
did you arm these sixty-five years
with a hatchet for our banishment?
And as you built the Soviet of God
did you plot these sixty-five years
with a millstone,
a spearhead,
and a horse?

Tunis, 24/7/1990

THE COLD

In this room
where the sky
descends, warning of rain . . .
in this room
where whiteness
sprinkles me with peelings
from the sloped ceiling,
I feel the coldness of graves.
A bone joint groans.
A spearhead sinks deeper.

Paris, 22/11/1990

ABDUCTION

That was not a country.
But it had all it needed
to imprint its image on us,
we the children of impossible clay.
That was not a country.
But it could erase the scrolls of our destiny.
Look how it rises in us again
and splits our blood like lightning!
We had forgotten it
and said we'll never see its papyrus,
not even in dreams.
We had forgotten it
the way soldiers forget first kisses,
the way a bed forgets the floor,
the way a wave forgets bottom moss.
We had forgotten it
and said we'll never see it again.
Who let it in through the window?
Who slipped it under the door?
Who brought it to us unaware
to abduct us
with its bloody hands
and to toss us
on top of a heap of meat
for vultures?

Paris, 5/5/1991

THE LOST LETTER

The dove will come
and I will watch her gyrations soar from here.
I will see the down from a distance —
white gray —
yawning under the flutter of her wings
as they land
here.
And I
from where I cannot be seen
will raise a prayer:
"Peace upon the tribe of birds wherever a wing lingers."

Perhaps I was raving. . . .
But the dove will come
for I am the one who best knows this earth and wind.
Even if I were blind here,
neglectful,
hermetic,
no one can see me. . . .
For seven years nothing has entered my hiding place,
no one
except what the soul sends
or whatever falls from my hands
through the tower windows,
grains
and water.

Paris, 26/10/1991

Damascus / Amman
1992–1997

ENDINGS

      A blind man
roams God's twenty-one villages
alone,
wearing his blindness like a treasure.
He strikes out in loss, and in loss his staff leads him.
Sometimes he fancies the earth his friend.
Wherever his feet end up
he is the drinker and the watering hole.
He looked into things about which he's never asked.
He is the first,
an indigent, a recluse,
and he is eternity.
. . . .
. . . .
. . . .

But God's twenty-one villages
are unjust. . . .
Someone may bury him alive in a well and conceal it.
Someone may choke him in a resting place.
Or wolves may claw him away from the women of the brothel.
So now
he must steady his steps
and race
            with dangers
to pass
            through terror . . .

Damascus, 9/12/1992

THE LIGHT

     Above the mountains of Aden,
on the top,
volcanic rocks moan with blackness
and the sea flies in mist.
Above the mountains of Aden,
exposed to wind and waves,
to maps drowned for centuries,
exposed to soldiers and towers,
there is a blind lighthouse.
. . . .
. . . .
. . . .

In the early morning Eurasian women
— thick hair under their armpits —
come near it.
Stumbling, unveiled, they scream the names
of men who were lost in a euphoria of guns
and potent liquors
and water . . .
. . . .
. . . .
. . . .

At night
waves approach the lighthouse slowly.
Lobsters whisper to it and magnificent turtles
and sharks.
. . . .
. . . .
. . . .

At night
in the bottom of the sea a sailor strides,
carrying a lantern he lit centuries ago.
He turns with the spiral staircase

stone
by stone
until he reaches the top.
And with the secrecy of night
he lights a blind lighthouse.

Damascus, 10/12/1992

SNOW MAY FALL

The room
is fortified with wooden blinds and glass,
and the lights
are off.
The pillows are quiet in their corners
and the paintings,
blue sky and yellow sand,
call forth all their intentions,
wishing away all I conceal.
There are trees across from the window
(the trees are always there).
Like a clever cat, the air sneaks in
under the door
to befriend me.
No wind whispers in the branches.
No bird flutters under a white sky.
No sound except music
coming from another earth.
But away from us
snow is filling its basket.
And surprisingly,
maybe tonight
snow will fall.

Amman, 22/12/1992

THE MOMENT

In the room
on the roof terrace facing the sea,
the retired pirate prepares his meal —
half a loaf of bread,
a slice of meat, a bottle of vodka. . . .
He shuts his door firmly
and from his ebony box
he takes out his ledgers,
his maps,
his harbors.
Now he's happy
and alone.
. . . .
. . . .
. . . .

But the chest rattles
and the eyes are small clouds.
. . . .
. . . .
. . . .

Who knocks on the door?
Who comes here following him
to this room on the roof?
The retired pirate closes his ebony box
and the secrets of his ledgers,
his maps,
his harbors,
and staggers a few steps
to drink up the scent of the sea.
. . . .
. . . .
. . . .

Could it be the blind one knocking on the door?
The blind one disguised as a woman coming
to befriend him at the moment his age is sealed?

Beirut, 14/4/1993

ON THE RED SEA

We were not sailors
but the captain's captives,
the sweepers of his kitchen. . . .
Sometimes he strolled
with his wolf dog
and we leapt in fright, terrified,
and fled to hide
in the corner of the stern.
The ship traveled by night,
folded its sails in the morning
at African ports,
and the sailors walked
to taverns on the beach.
As for us
we remained as we were,
the captain's captives,
the sweepers of his kitchen . . .

Amman, 30/6/1993

ATTENTION

Those who come by me passing,
I will remember them,
and those who come heavy and overbearing,
I will forget.
. . . .
. . . .
. . . .
This is why
when air gushes between mountains
we describe the wind
and forget the rocks.

Amman, 8/7/1993

FOR JAMAL JUMAA

Finally . . .
if you sit on top of the earth's sphere,
happily dangling your feet, flayed from roving,
ready to write poems,
remember there is someone who wishes
to make a seat out of your skull
and to dangle his scaly feet on your chest
to muffle the first wails of poetry.

Amman, 11/7/1993

THE KURDISH QUARTER

First: the cat wakes
even before the swifts lunge into the dance
between roof and wind. . . .
The cat,
warlike,
her tail bristling,
is intent on hunting. . . .
The bird on top of the electricity pole
or the cockroach by the drain.
Or a bounty might befall her this morning:
a mouse may pass by. . . .

Second: the lights at the foot of the mountain are put out,
house by house . . . and the night witch disappears.
The barren mountain sends its first dust
and the tin sky
and things we do not know. . . .

Third: the Kurd awakes on the roof
and quietly folds what he spread for a bed last night.
He leaves nothing there
except his wide pants
bloating,
fluttering
on the washline . . .

Damascus, 22/2/1994

THE HERMIT

1.

The poets leave
one after the other at the end of the night.
They carry nothing but pollen
and open-return tickets.
I tell them: "Don't quicken your steps.
Brothers, wait another hour.
We're at the end of the night."
But they leave.

The sky is not pitch black. Only clouds fall deeply. . . .
Black, they seem, and gray. Dawn is leery, yet it is
still dawn. To a constant white cloud in the corner of
the sky I say: "You are mine, my crescent-shaped radiance.
I waited for you all
night while you were under my pillow,
pulling at my hairs and caressing. You will stay with me.
Wherever I am, you will be." I will say: "The sky is clear."
I will proclaim you daylight.
Good morning, dear boy.

2.

The poets leave
one after the other at the end of a verse. . . .
How did you end up at point zero?
How did you end up here?
Where did you leave our lanterns, the mountaintops?
Have you never watched the eyes of cats?
Have we reached the end of the line?
Yet you still leave.

This mountain will not be hemmed. This mountain we know.
From its shacks we will bring honey and eagle droppings.
The flowers are without names. And the threadbare spring, and the
    wolves
that sniff for village smells. There are passageways, goat paths,
and smugglers. The soldiers are not guests here. The saint's
grave is blessed with green ribbons. And from houses we do not
    know women
and children come with candles and bread.
Good morning, dear mountain!

   3.

The poets leave
one after the other at the end of a branch.
No!
How can you leave me?
Did we not gather around tables of drink?
We used to say: "The ripples on the water are ours."
We used to say: "The branches are ours and the golden autumn."
And say: "The tip of the branch."
Yet you leave.

Tree, you are blessed. Flowering, you are blessed
with peacock feathers and a hoopoe's crest. Blessed are your roots
where ants lay their eggs. The porcupine circles you following
the star, and from your branches grasshoppers chirp. In silvery white
    night
you fan yourself with air from paradise. And in golden daylight
you distill silver. I will say: "You're my first tree.
My hut and my tomb and the crown I wear."
Good morning, poetry.

4.

I will not blame you.
I will not say good-bye through the wasteland of alcohol.
I will not bend when the storm erupts.
I will repeat your names . . .
and your skies.
I will be the trusted guard over what you left behind.
I will be the prince of dust.

5.

At night,
at the end of the night,
birds will come to me
and the prairie wolves will come wet with dew
and the gazelle will come.

At the end of the night,
seven poets will take refuge in my cave . . .

Amman, 29/11/1994

AMERICA, AMERICA

God save America,
My home, sweet home!

The French general who raised his tricolor
over Nuqrat al-Salman where I was a prisoner
thirty years ago . . .
in the middle of that U-turn
that split the back of the Iraqi army,
the general who loved Saint Emilion wines
called Nuqrat al-Salman a fort . . . .
Of the surface of the earth, generals know only two dimensions:
whatever rises is a fort,
whatever spreads is a battlefield.
How ignorant the general was!
But *Liberation* was better versed in topography.
The Iraqi boy who conquered her front page
sat carbonized behind a steering wheel
on the Kuwait-Safwan highway
while television cameras
(the booty of the defeated and their identity)
were safe in a truck like a storefront
on Rivoli Street.
The neutron bomb is highly intelligent.
It distinguishes between
an "I" and an "Identity."

God save America,
My home, sweet home!

Blues
How long must I walk to Sacramento?
How long must I walk to Sacramento?
How long will I walk to reach my home?
How long will I walk to reach my girl?

How long must I walk to Sacramento?
For two days, no boat has sailed this stream,
Two days, two days, two days.

Honey, how can I ride?
I know this stream,
But, O but, O but,
For two days, no boat has sailed this stream.

La Li La La Li La
La Li La La Li La
A stranger becomes afraid.
Have no fear, dear horse.
No fear of the wolves of the wild,
No fear, for the land is my land.
La Li La La Li La
La Li La La Li La
A stranger becomes afraid.

God save America,
My home, sweet home!

I too love jeans and jazz and *Treasure Island*
and John Silver's parrot and the balconies of New Orleans.
I love Mark Twain and the Mississippi steamboats and Abraham
    Lincoln's dogs.
I love the fields of wheat and corn and the smell of Virginia tobacco.
But I am not American.
Is that enough for the Phantom pilot to turn me back to the Stone
    Age?
I need neither oil nor America herself, neither the elephant nor the
    donkey.

Leave me, pilot, leave my house roofed with palm fronds and this
    wooden bridge.
I need neither your Golden Gate nor your skyscrapers.
I need the village, not New York.
Why did you come to me from your Nevada desert, soldier armed to
    the teeth?
Why did you come all the way to distant Basra, where fish used to
    swim by our doorsteps?
Pigs do not forage here.
I only have these water buffaloes lazily chewing on water lilies.
Leave me alone, soldier.
Leave me my floating cane hut and my fishing spear.
Leave me my migrating birds and the green plumes.
Take your roaring iron birds and your Tomahawk missiles. I am not
    your foe.
I am the one who wades up to the knees in rice paddies.
Leave me to my curse.
I do not need your day of doom.

God save America,
My home, sweet home!

America:
let's exchange gifts.
Take your smuggled cigarettes
and give us potatoes.
Take James Bond's golden pistol
and give us Marilyn Monroe's giggle.
Take the heroin syringe under the tree
and give us vaccines.
Take your blueprints for model penitentiaries
and give us village homes.
Take the books of your missionaries

and give us paper for poems to defame you.
Take what you do not have
and give us what we have.
Take the stripes of your flag
and give us the stars.
Take the Afghani mujahideen beard
and give us Walt Whitman's beard filled with butterflies.
Take Saddam Hussein
and give us Abraham Lincoln
or give us no one.

Now as I look across the balcony,
across the summer sky, the summery summer,
Damascus spins, dizzied among television aerials,
then it sinks, deeply, in the stones of the forts,
                    in towers,
                    in the arabesques of ivory,
and sinks, deeply, far from Rukn el-Din
and disappears far from the balcony.

And now
I remember trees:
the date palm of our mosque in Basra, at the end of Basra
a bird's beak,
a child's secret,
a summer feast.
I remember the date palm.
I touch it. I become it, when it falls black
without fronds,
when a dam fell, hewn by lightning.
And I remember the mighty mulberry
when it rumbled, butchered with an axe . . .
to fill the stream with leaves

and birds
and angels
and green blood.
I remember when pomegranate blossoms covered the sidewalks.
The students were leading the workers parade. . . .

The trees die
pummeled.
Dizzied,
not standing, the trees die.

> *God save America,*
> *My home, sweet home!*

We are not hostages, America,
and your soldiers are not God's soldiers. . . .
We are the poor ones, ours is the earth of the drowned gods,
the gods of bulls,
the gods of fires,
the gods of sorrows that intertwine clay and blood in a song. . . .
We are the poor, ours is the god of the poor,
who emerges out of farmers' ribs,
hungry
and bright,
and raises heads up high. . . .

America, we are the dead.
Let your soldiers come.
Whoever kills a man, let him resurrect him.
We are the drowned ones, dear lady.
We are the drowned.
Let the water come.

Damascus, 20/8/1995

THE ATTEMPT

Philip the Macedonian
was the fastest man to answer a question.
He said: "I will remain by the sword.
And I will sleep by the sword —
even if my bones are bleached white —
so long as the sword remains."

But Alexander
did not learn what a son learns
from a father.
He said:
"I will roam the world.
My companions will be
warriors and philosophers
and I will seek answers to
the world's questions."

Alexander
wandered, burning
with the world's questions.
But he remained alone,
without a grave,
and remained distant. . . .
He left only his image:
the face of a boy
who tried to look the world in the face.

Cairo, 12/11/1996

TRYING TO FLEE

How can I travel to Tangier this evening?
(At night one remembers his best days.)
A street with a name unknown to me,
a neighborhood I didn't visit,
a shirt I wish I had unbuttoned.

The garden is all dried up
and the evening here is lonely.
The stars fluttering above are blue in the chill.
How can I travel this evening?

How can I travel to Costa Rica?
(At night one remembers his sweetest friendships.)
I have a friend there
who gathers his identity papers every day
to read in them the country he never loved . . .
the country he may have loved,
the country where everything is ash. . . .
How can I travel this evening?

How can I travel to my room this evening?
(At night one remembers his quietest places.)
I have never had, if you want the truth, a house or a room.
But I need a place
where only my pulse can enter,
where the air is unlike this air,
a room that is never lit
but never overtaken by darkness.

A room in space. . . .

How can I travel this evening?

Amman, 6/3/1997

A VISION

This Iraq will reach the ends of the graveyard.
It will bury its sons in open country
generation after generation,
and it will forgive its despot. . . .
It will not be the Iraq that once held the name.
And the larks will not sing.
So walk — if you wish — a long time.
And call — if you wish —
on all the world's angels
and all its demons.
Call on the bulls of Assyria.
Call on a westward phoenix. . . .
Call them
and through the haze of phantoms
watch for miracles to emerge
from clouds of incense.

Amman, 8/3/1997

HAPPINESS

To fill your eyes
there are rose shrubs
and branches of a lemon tree.

The stone houses
you once hated
rise higher and higher,
wet with rain.

Thinking is not enough.

O
happy is a man
who opens a window
unto the morning!

Amman, 24/3/1997

NOTES

"Three Stories from Kuwait":

Safwan and Matlaa are the border towns on the Kuwait-Iraq border.
"Safwan to Matlaa!" is the chant of intercity taxi drivers calling on
passengers.

Zaatar, a Palestinian delicacy, is a mixture of ground herbs (mostly thyme)
eaten with olive oil and bread.

"Shatt al Arab":

Shatt al Arab is the estuary formed at the convergence of the Tigris and
Euphrates in southern Iraq. Ahwaz is a region on the southern borders of
Iran and Iraq.

"The Ends of the African North":

The "five-angled disc" is a reference to a five-point star in the flag of
Morocco.

According to the poet, the phrase "tertiary face" refers to the three major
political currents in Iraq at mid-century: nationalist Baathists,
Communists, and Monarchists.

"L'Akhdar Ben Youssef and His Concerns":

"Eid" refers to two of the holiest days in the Islamic calendar, Eid al-Fitr,
which celebrates the end of the fasting month of Ramadan, and Eid
al-Adha (the feast of sacrifice), which celebrates the Quranic story of
Ibrahim and Ismail and the end of the pilgrimage season to Mecca.

"In Those Days":

The third of May is the anniversary of the poet's conviction and subsequent
imprisonment for political activities in Iraq.

"On L'Akhdar Again":

The "Qarawites" refers to an ancient university of Islamic sciences located
in Fez, Morocco. The "Alawites" refers to the name of the royal family cur-
rently ruling Morocco.

"How L'Akhdar Ben Youssef Wrote His Last Poem":

"Search for your defeated ring in your victorious country" is an allusion to a line by the Arab poet al-Mutannabi (915–965). A later line in this poem explains Mutannabi's image of a myopic man looking for his ring in the sand.

"Enemies":

The image of the quails and manna is a biblical as well as a Quranic allusion. In Arabic the poet uses the word *salwa*, referring to the quails sent by God to the children of Israel during their forty years in the desert. Connotatively, *salwa* has come to mean "consolation," much more so than as a signifier for "quails." Thus, in the poem the poet manages to evoke both senses of the word to refer to something being sent by a higher power. The "paper quails" the poet refers to later in the poem are leaflets being tossed from a plane. In a later line I translate *salwa* as "consolation" to evoke that second meaning as well.

Sibah is a detention center in Iraq where the poet was held in the 1960s.

"The Spring":

Dhafar is a region in Oman where a leftist rebellion took place in the 1970s and was quelled. Najd is a region in Saudi Arabia. Al-Hallaj (858–922) was a medieval mystic poet who was accused of heresy and executed. Fakhani is a neighborhood in Beirut. Damur is a Palestinian refugee camp in Lebanon. Samarra is a city north of Baghdad famed for its spiral tower, one of the jewels of medieval Islamic architecture. Lahaj and Mukalla are cities in Yemen. Hadramout is a region in Yemen. Dammoun is a region in southern Arabia mentioned in a poem by Imru ul-Qais.

"A Friendship":

Ibn Taymiya (1263–1328) was an archconservative Muslim scholar who brought about a retrenchment in Islamic jurisprudence. Known as the resuscitator of the sunna (the prophetic tradition and practices), he is highly admired by contemporary Muslim fundamentalists. Al-Muwafaq was an Abbasid Caliph during whose reign a major slave rebellion took place.

"Days of June":

Khalil Hawi was a prominent Lebanese poet who committed suicide during the Israeli siege and bombardment of Beirut in the summer of 1982. "Sinnin" is Mount Sinnin, the highest mountain in Lebanon. The line "Isn't she the one who slipped away from Cherbourg one evening" refers to French naval frigates made in Cherbourg, France, that aided Israel during its wars with its Arab neighbors.

"Maryam Comes":

Lailki and Sullam are neighborhoods in Beirut.

"Thank You Imru ul-Qais":

Imru ul-Qais (?–530) is one of the great Arab pre-Islamic poets, author of one of the seven suspended odes. He was a prince of the people of Kinda. He is known as the wandering prince, first because he was expelled by his father as punishment for his amorous passions, the embarrassment his poetry had caused, and also because of his father's murder. The poet began a career of wandering, living the life of a dethroned king, seeking means to reestablish his father's power, which he never recovered. Toward the end of his life, he was appointed Phylarch of Jerusalem by the Byzantine Emperor Justinian. But soon afterward he died at Ancyra, poisoned on the emperor's order, and, the legend runs, by a garment of honor, a robe of Nessus which covered his body with ulcers, as punishment for seducing a royal lady.

"The Trees of Ithaca":

Sullam, Alhamra, and Barbir are neighborhoods in Beirut. Al-Mathaf is a district in Beirut named after the museum where a great deal of civil-war fighting took place. Khalda is an area in Beirut where a tank battle took place during the Israeli invasion of 1982.

The names listed at the end of some stanzas are of Palestinian heroes, living and martyred. In the last list the poet adds the name of al-Khidr, who is a mythological spiritual figure known throughout the Islamic world. Readers of the Quran assume that he is one of the knowledgeable servants of God upon whom certain powers were endowed (see Quran 18:64). Al-Khidr literally means "the green one." Considered a guide to prophets and capable of transcending time and space, he is a central figure in Sufi lore as a symbol of the ancient and ever-present metaphysical intellect. Enigmatic, but firmly associated with virtue, he exists between the seen and the unseen.

"America, America":

In the poem's main refrain the poet (possibly unintentionally) collapses the American "God bless America" with the British "God save the Queen." In the poem, the line appears in English.

Rukn el-Din is a neighborhood in Damascus.

SAADI YOUSSEF was born in 1934 in Basra, Iraq. He has published thirty volumes of poetry, seven books of prose, and has rendered into Arabic major works by such writers as Walt Whitman, Constantine Cavafy, Federico García Lorca, George Orwell, Nuruddin Farah, and Wole Soyinka. He left Iraq in 1979, and after many detours, working as a journalist, publisher, and political activist, he has recently settled in London.

KHALED MATTAWA is the author of a collection of poetry, *Ismailia Eclipse,* and the translator of two books of contemporary Arabic poetry, Hatif Janabi's *Questions and Their Retinue* and Fadhil al-Azzawi's *In Every Well a Joseph Is Weeping.* He currently teaches at the University of Texas at Austin.

The text of this book has been set in Adobe Caslon, a typeface drawn by Carol Twombly in 1989 and based on the work of William Caslon, who designed and cut a large number of romans, italics, and non-Latin faces between 1720 and 1766. He is considered by many to be the first great English typecutter.

Book design and composition by Wendy Holdman at Stanton Publication Services, Inc., St. Paul, Minnesota. Manufactured by Bang Printing on acid-free paper.

Graywolf Press is a not-for-profit, independent press. The books we publish include poetry, literary fiction, and cultural criticism. We are less interested in best-sellers than in talented writers who display a freshness of voice coupled with a distinct vision. We believe these are the very qualities essential to shape a vital and diverse culture.

Thankfully, many of our readers feel the same way. They have shown this through their desire to buy books by Graywolf writers; they have told us this themselves through their e-mail notes and at author events; and they have reinforced their commitment by contributing financial support, in small amounts and in large amounts, and joining the "Friends of Graywolf."

If you enjoyed this book and wish to learn more about Graywolf Press, we invite you to ask your bookseller or librarian about further Graywolf titles; or to contact us for a free catalog; or to visit our award-winning web site that features information about our forthcoming books.

We would also like to invite you to consider joining the hundreds of individuals who are already "Friends of Graywolf" by contributing to our membership program. Individual donations of any size are significant to us: they tell us that you believe that the kind of publishing we do *matters*. Our web site gives you many more details about the benefits you will enjoy as a "Friend of Graywolf"; but if you do not have online access, we urge you to contact us for a copy of our membership brochure.

www.graywolfpress.org

Graywolf Press
2402 University Avenue, Suite 203
Saint Paul, MN 55114
Phone: (651) 641-0077
Fax: (651) 641-0036
E-mail: wolves@graywolfpress.org

Other Graywolf titles you might enjoy are:

No Shelter: The Selected Poems of Pura López-Colomé,
    translated by Forrest Gander

The Half-Finished Heaven: The Best Poems of Tomas Tranströmer,
    chosen and translated by Robert Bly

The Horse Has Six Legs: An Anthology of Serbian Poetry,
    translated by Charles Simic

The Complete French Poems of Rainer María Rilke,
    translated by A. Poulin, Jr.

The Way It Is: New & Selected Poems
    by William Stafford